You Don't Need Bruises to be Abused

You Don't Need Bruises to be Abused

Brian Fox

PNEUMA SPRINGS PUBLISHING UK

First Published 2008
Published by Pneuma Springs Publishing

You Don't Need Bruises to be Abused
Copyright © 2008 Brian Fox
E:brian@smellthereality.com
W:www.smellthereality.com

ISBN: 978-1-905809-20-2

Cover design, editing and typesetting by:
Pneuma Springs Publishing

A Subsidiary of Pneuma Springs Ltd.
7 Groveherst Road, Dartford Kent, DA1 5JD.
E: admin@pneumasprings.co.uk
W: www.pneumasprings.co.uk

A catalogue record for this book is available from the British Library.

Published in the United Kingdom. All rights reserved under International Copyright Law. Contents and/or cover may not be reproduced in whole or in part without the express written consent of the publisher.

DEDICATION

For my beautiful wife Ange

Against all the odds she has become a beacon of light and hope in my life and has taught me the real meaning of strength and courage.

Acknowledgements

Throughout this book I make reference to a television show called 'Keeping Up Appearances". I use this show to provide common examples and not to pass judgement on anyone involved with it. This show is written by Roy Clarke, and I can only say that I find the show very amusing and entertaining.

Mum and Dad who are always there, always supportive, always loving and always loved. Thank You!

Foreword

I have been reading a book about September 11 and the World Trade Centre and at the same time we have had a lot of news going on with regards to terrorist and terrorism. People are outraged at how people can use intimidation, violence, coercion and manipulation to force others to their way of thinking. And you know, rightly so; people should be outraged that this kind of thing is going on in the world today.

Having just finished writing a booklet called "Why don't they just leave?", (available for free download from www.smellthereality.com) which is where some of the ideas for this book came from, I started thinking about domestic abuse and I realised that although terrorism (as we know it), is relatively new, it is going on around us each and every day.

The role of an abuser in a situation of domestic abuse is exactly the same as in terrorism; in that they are imposing their will and ideas on another person by violence, fear, coercion and manipulation. That makes them terrorists, and that is not acceptable to anyone.

Even though it is on a different scale, it is still happening, and it is happening in huge numbers. It is happening to people we know; our friends, our family, and our neighbours. You would be surprised to find out how rampant abuse is in our society today.

I first came across domestic abuse in reality about five years ago, and since then it amazes me just how big a problem this still is in the world today. Just to be clear I am talking about typical western society, not cultures that may have a very different view on things. I am talking about European, American, British, etc. societies where people are all supposed to be treated as equals in every sense of the word.

Domestic abuse is not confined to any class of people. It does not have limits in lower income families, it is not only something that happens in the movies; it is everywhere.

The reason I am writing this book is because I have gained some insight into what is going on below the surface in these environments. I obviously do not know all the details of what goes on in all the specific instances but I do know a lot about people. How they think generally and what goes on in a domestic abuse situation.

I am not a psychologist and I am not a psychiatrist; I am someone who devotes their time and energies working with real people in the real world. I do not have a load of psycho-babble up my sleeve so that I can dazzle you with my intellect.

I am writing this book because I believe that the things that I have to say are worth saying and they are worth hearing. If you or someone you know is stuck in a domestic abuse situation then I hope that you will learn something from this and that it will help you make a difference. That is what this book is all about; making a difference to people.

This is my third book; the others being "Wake Up and Smell the Reality!" which is a self-help book aimed at helping people change their lives by themselves. The second book is called "Creating Adults; NOT Raising Children (Weighing up the Autistic Scale)" This book is aimed at helping parents in general, but more specifically those with children with ADD, ADHD and Aspergers Syndrome.

The ideas and thoughts in this book have been developed over several years. They are my views and they are not written here as anything other than my thoughts and ideas. I am not a professional in this area, but I think that you will find that the things in here simply make sense.

The thing with all of my works is that they are designed to at least provoke thought. I do not have all of the answers, however I would like to think that whilst you are reading through this you would at least begin to think deeply about the issues discussed here and you will start learning something about what is going on. If you can take the things that you learn from me, add your own ideas to it and then change yours, or someone else's life for the better then I have done my job.

As always I am interested in any thoughts or feedback that you have. I can be reached through our website www.smellthereality.com

I do hope that you will get something from this book.

Contents

The First Bit..19

Ange's Story – In a Nutshell 20

Introduction.. 22

Rights in a relationship.................................. 25

The Power of Words...................................... 27

You don't need bruises to be abused........... 29

    Physical Abuse... 30

    Manipulation.. 31

    Verbal Abuse.. 33

    Isolation... 34

    Financial Dependency............................ 35

    Blackmail... 36

    Fear (of Physical Abuse)......................... 37

    Jealousy... 38

    Infidelity.. 39

    Stripping of self-respect and dignity.... 39

    It all leads to control............................... 40

    Any/ALL of the above............................ 42

When does it become abuse?........................ 43

Why don't they just leave?........................... 46

Ignorance and Expectations.......................... 49

How does it happen in the First Place?...... 51

Where is the control?..................................... 55

What is tolerated is validated....................... 57

- Power has to be given as well as taken...................60
- The Conveyer Belt..62
- Behind Closed Doors..65

End of Section..67

The Victim..68
- Denial, Hope and Excuses.....................................71
  - Denial...71
  - Hope..73
  - Excuses..75
  - Summary..76
- The Blame Game..78
- Fear, Fear and more Fear......................................81
  - Fear of Danger from Abuser..............................82
  - Fear for the children..83
  - Fear for others...84
  - Fear of retribution from others besides the abuser....85
  - Fear of failing in the relationship.....................86
  - Fear of being alone..87
  - Fear of not being good enough without them..........88
  - Fear of looking like a fool.................................89
  - Fear of the unknown..90
  - Summary..90
- Comfort Zones..93
- What's left when your self-respect is taken?......96
- Failure is a big part of the picture.....................99

Pride – Enemy and Saviour.................................102
What about the Kids...105
    Parenting in an Abusive Situation....................105
    What they are being taught...............................107
    Does the victim have more than one abuser?..........108
    Two Parents don't always mean it is better............109
Barriers...111
Survival Mode..116
It no longer even occurs to them to leave..............118
Some People are always Victims............................120
Something for the victim to think about 123

End of Section...128

To The Abuser...131
Do you know what you are doing?.......................133
How can you mistreat someone you love?............135
Where does it start?...137
Where does it end?..139
Excuses, Excuses, Excuses...................................141
Old Fashioned is not an excuse............................143
It is not the victim's fault....................................145
What about the kids...147
No! It is not your right.......................................149
If you don't like the victim, why don't you leave?.......150
What do you tell your friends?............................152
Where has the respect and love gone?..................153

    Where is it going, on the current course? 155
    Time to take responsibility............................. 157
    The Guy in the Glass.. 159

End of Section.. 160

How You Can Help... 161
    Being a friend.. 163
    Understand what is really happening............... 165
    Don't push too hard.. 167
    Don't get involved in the blame game............. 170
    It has to come from Self Awareness................. 171
    They do still have options................................. 173
    Support, Support and Support.......................... 176
    Don't help them wallow in their misery......... 178
    Don't give up.. 179
    Some Practical things you can do..................... 181
        Keep a diary... 181
        Provide distractions..................................... 181
        Provide Information.................................... 182
        Smile and Nod... 182
        Where can they get help?........................... 183

End of the Section... 85

To The Victim.. 187
    Life in a black hole... 189
    You are more than a victim............................... 191
    Don't think like a victim................................... 194
    You do deserve to have better........................... 200

Think about what you owe.................................204
It is not your fault.................................207
I hope I am not scaring you.................................212
Control is in the mind.................................215
Dealing with Fear.................................219
Five years from now.................................222
    Option one.................................223
    Option two.................................223
    Other options.................................224
How do you make the move?.................................226
What happens after the move?.................................230
Moving out has to mean moving on.................................234
Revenge is not the answer.................................239
Are they still controlling your life?.................................243
Think and Grow.................................246

End of Section.................................247

The Last Bit.................................249

At the end of the day.................................249

THE FIRST BIT

Welcome to the first bit. When putting this book together it seemed the best way to do it would be to put different bits into separate sections. The trouble I had was what to call the first part, so I decided that as it was the first bit in the book; that is what I would call it.

In this section I will be defining a lot of terms and setting some of the ground rules for the entire book. I will talk a little about the other sections in the introduction, but before that I am including a chapter called Ange's Story – In a Nutshell.

Ange is my wife, however before we got together she had a very different life, and I wanted to include a brief overview of her story to demonstrate a number of things, including the fact that there is light at the end of the tunnel, and that it is never too late. This is very much a summary of the story, as I hope to write the story in full in another book; so watch out for it in the shops – one day. With all that in mind, we can get on with the rest of the book.

Ange's Story – In a Nutshell

It was about 5 years ago that I came to know Ange, who is now my wife. At that time she was married to another man and was involved in a very manipulative and abusive relationship. That relationship had been going on for about 15 years and ended finally with Ange going to the police and having him charged with rape. Ultimately he was found guilty of 5 counts and was sentenced to 5 years in prison. If you think about it, a husband being convicted of raping his wife is a very serious thing. To be convicted on five counts is even more gruesome. If you put it into perspective, that is only the five incidents that could be proved; all of the other rapes went unnoticed.

When I first encountered Ange she was nothing like the person that she is today. She was someone who was timid and shy. She had no self-respect and no real zest for life. For her, life was all about surviving each day and getting through the best she could.

She had two children and a husband who was a very heavy drinker. He kept Ange without money, without friends, and without dignity. The whole world essentially revolved around him. To him everything was second to his needs and wants, and that included the kids.

As far as he was concerned, Ange and the kids were simply his possessions that he would bring out when he wanted to make an impression; otherwise they were there merely to serve him. He did not allow them to get in the way of his life in any way.

Before Ange came home she would literally stop at the front gate, take a deep breath and steady herself for even walking in the front door. It got so bad that Ange was ready to end her life. Obviously she did not do that, instead she took action to make changes that would change her life forever.

It does take a lot to go from the moment of being ready to end your life, to rising up and changing it. For Ange to be able to finally get the courage to do something about it took a huge amount of strength and determination, against the odds. It took strength to be able to claw back her self-respect and dignity and to start realising that this is not the way that her life was meant to be.

In the last four years, since Ange finally made the changes to her life, she has gone from strength to strength. She is working for Social Services as well as working as a personal mentor, helping others to do what she has done. She has returned to college and successfully completed several subjects.

She is no longer the shy timid person that I first encountered. She is strong and vibrant and walks through life with a spring in her step, a sparkle in her eye and enjoys her life.

INTRODUCTION

Domestic abuse comes in many shapes and forms and is as wide spread today as it has ever been. The title of this book tells you that you don't need bruises to be abused. What that means is that it is not just the victims of physical violence that are being abused.

Throughout this book we will be looking at what is really going on beneath the surface; what that means is that we will look at the effects that abuse has on the victim. The reason for this is that it will give you a different view of what is happening and will help answer the long-standing question of – Why don't they just leave?

The answer to that question is complicated beyond belief as there are so many factors that involve not only the physical but also the mental and emotional damage that goes on. In fact it would be fair to say that the physical damage, if in fact there is any, is perhaps the smallest part of the consideration.

There are a few things that I want to make sure we are clear about before we get into the depths of the book. There are many misconceptions about abusive relationships, the primary one being that that it is the male that is always the abuser. This is very far from the truth. Keeping in mind that abuse is much more than bruises, there are many men that are abused, manipulated and controlled by their partners. Throughout this book I will refer to the abuser and the victim, it should never be taken that the victim is always a woman and the abuser a man; that simply is not the truth.

The other thing that we need to be clear on is what type of relationship we are dealing with. In this book we are talking about a relationship between two parties, being essentially partners. It does not mean that they are married, or even living together. There are many different types of relationship, and the abuse can start even before a commitment such as living together and marriage is considered. It would also be fair to say that relationships are not confined to be strictly male and female; the people in the relationship could also be the same gender.

It is important to keep in mind that all relationships are as different as the people that are involved in them. The information provided here is based on essentially general information. It is designed to make you think about the relationship and what is going on below the surface. It is the ideas that are presented here and how they apply to you that is crucial.

This book does not deal directly with domestic abuse in the sense of abused children; however a lot of the mental and emotional abuse that is talked about here is relevant to some degree.

Essentially the purpose of this book is to provide information and insight into what is going on at many different levels. By itself it is not going to solve the problem of domestic abuse, but the idea is that if you understand something better then you are better able to do something about it.

This book is broken down into sections in order to give some order to the thoughts that are presented. The first section essentially sets the scene and describes in a lot more detail the subject of abuse.

The second section takes a closer look at the victim and what is going on within them. The idea is to look at what is going on inside the minds of the people involved. Once again, there is so much more to being in an abusive relationship than is obvious to everyone.

The third section examines the abuser and tries to understand what is going on in their mind and also offers some ideas, thoughts and suggestions that will be useful to everyone reading this book.

The forth section touches on what a third party who is on the outside can do to help the situation. There are many things that need to be taken into consideration when trying to help someone who is stuck in an abusive relationship; these will be discussed in this section.

The fifth section talks to the victim and offers them help to make the move and talks about what happens after an abusive relationship. It is all about how to move forward and begin a new life.

The last section is the summary and a bit more waffling from me.

RIGHTS IN A RELATIONSHIP

There can be a little confusion about what rights a person has in a relationship, so I thought I would try and clear that up. Quite simply a person has the same rights in a relationship as they would at any other time.

What that means is that regardless of gender, age, upbringing or any other factors, an individual has the right to be treated as an equal. A great deal of our notion of relationships originally came from a gender biased history. What this means is that our parents and our grandparents had a different idea about the individual rights in a relationship when compared to what we have today.

If you were walking down the street and someone came along and started abusing you physically or mentally then you would report it to the police. The same applies to a partner in a relationship; they simply do not have the right to do that to anyone, despite what they may tell the victim.

A person's body is theirs, and nobody has rights to use it in any way that they don't want them to. Rape is still rape, regardless if it is within a relationship or not. They have every right to say no. Sex without consent is rape; it does not get any simpler than that.

When two people come together there are obviously different personalities that are involved. Some people are more dominant than others and may therefore take a leading role in the relationship, but if this is not done with respect, care and thought for the other party, then it is starting to get into the realms of abuse.

A relationship is a joining of equals and both parties have equal rights in the relationship. When in a relationship you are still an individual. You have the right to expect everything you should as if you were single. No one has a right to mistreat, demean, threaten, hurt or take advantage of another person, regardless of relationships.

My Mum always told me to do to others as I would like to be done to me. It applies in this situation, in that if you are not being treated the way that you would treat another person, perhaps it is time to have a look at the situation.

There are many examples that I could use to make this point, but I want to keep it as simple as possible and that is – you have the same rights in a relationship as you do by simply being a person.

Don't allow anyone to tell you anything different and don't allow anyone to take your rights away from you.

THE POWER OF WORDS

In order to talk about the different types of domestic abuse and the fact that you do not need bruises to be abused, I thought it would be a good idea to look at the power of words, and how they affect us; far beyond anything that most people ever realise.

I am going to start out on a very philosophical track here in that I am going to talk about words and the power that they posses. It is one of those things that we use every day for many different purposes, and yet it is very rare that we actually stop to think about the power that we have at our disposal; some more than others, but it is infinite power nonetheless.

Let's take an example in the book that you are now reading. All of the ideas, thoughts and messages are given to you in words. It is through the power of words that you are able to read this book, form you own version of the ideas and thoughts that are presented here. From there you will form your own opinions on things in your world that you relate the ideas in this book to, and now comes the key point, you will act accordingly.

Let's take a quick look at a simple example of the power of words. If I was to say to someone 'You are worthless, fat and lazy, if you did not have me; then nobody would have you; you should just be grateful that I am here to take care of you'.

Now that is a pretty devastating thing to hear. Imagine if it was said to you over and over again. It is going to start becoming a controlling factor in your life. It is powerful because it triggers emotions and responses; that is where the power lies.

The same as if I was to say to someone 'You are a beautiful person and a hard worker. I am very proud of you and I am glad that you choose to be with me.'

Again, there is a lot that is said in that sentence and it will still trigger an emotional response, but it is a very different one. That is the power of words, and how they can be used. The power of words really is limitless and that is one of the things that will become very clear as we continue to look at the subject of abuse.

Having said all this about the power of words, I am going to take this one step further by saying it is not the words themselves that have the power, it is what they mean and what results from them that actually holds the power. A quick example of this is a word as simple as 'Yes'. This is a word that we use all the time, but it means so many different things, depending on the question that is asked. Essentially when you use this word, you are agreeing to whatever has been asked; you are now committed to whatever result is going to happen, because you have agreed to it. I think it is important to be aware of this concept, as it plays a huge part in the things we are going to be discussing throughout the rest of this book. But for now we will just keep in mind that words have enormous power.

What I am trying to say in this chapter is that although they are only words, and we have all heard of 'stick and stones will break my bones; but words will never hurt me', I am going to tell you that there is nothing further from the truth. Sure sticks and stones will hurt and could break bones, but unless they are fatal, they will heal and you will carry on. It is words that inflict wounds that go far beyond the physical and get into the mental and emotional realm and once you are wounded there, it takes more than a band-aid to heal it.

I think the saying mentioned above should be changed to say something like 'sticks and stones may break my bones, but harsh words can really destroy me'. This is closer to the truth.

YOU DON'T NEED BRUISES TO BE ABUSED

Usually when someone thinks about domestic abuse the first thing they think of is violence. But there are so many other ways that someone can be abusive that I have to say that violence is really a small part of it. Stay with me here; I am not trying to diminish the physical violence at all, what I am saying here is that if there is violence, then that is just the tip of the iceberg.

If you look at a relationship that is violent, even the violence is typically a small part of the whole problem. If someone is violent to another person it is generally used as a form of control. However you do not need violence to gain control over another person. Control is not gained only physically, it can also be gained by mental and/or emotional means.

Abuse can come in many different forms, all of which essentially lead to control. That is the aim of the abuser, to have control over the victim to the point where they get what they want when they want it. It may not start out like that, but ultimately that is where it ends up. Once they have control, the object then is to keep it. They want it all their own way, and they usually end up getting it.

To gain control an abuser will use many different tools and more than likely they will user a number of them at the same time. Manipulation, isolation, fear, threat, belittling, degrading etc. They essentially strip the victim of self confidence, self-respect and self-worth. All these are forms of abuse that do not leave bruises, at least not on the body.

Abuse is defined on www.dictionary.com as follows:

1. to use wrongly or improperly; misuse
2. to treat in a harmful, injurious, or offensive way
3. to speak insultingly, harshly, and unjustly to or about; revile; malign
4. to commit sexual assault upon

5. wrong or improper use; misuse
6. harshly or coarsely insulting language
7. bad or improper treatment; maltreatment
8. a corrupt or improper practice or custom

As you can see by the definitions, there is only one of the eight that even mentions violence. To be an abuser does not mean that you have to be physically stronger, it simply means that one person is in control of the other person and using that control for personal gains regardless of the victim.

Another way to look at an abuser is as a bully. A school yard bully is essentially the same thing. They use intimidation, fear and manipulation to get control over the victim, for their own personal gain. As mentioned earlier this is also the same as a terrorist, albeit on a different scale. When you live with the bully and almost your entire life is being controlled, then it becomes an even bigger problem.

I hope that I have made it clear here that it is not just the bruises that make someone a victim. There are many ways in which abuse manifests itself within a relationship. We are going to talk about this some more, but for now I just wanted to make the point that there is so much more to being abused than the violence, in fact you don't even need the violence in the first place.

In the next section we will go into a little more detail just to give more insight into abuse and to make sure we are clear about this subject matter.

Physical Abuse

When domestic abuse is mentioned, the first thought is always that there is violence and physical abuse going on. I think this is generally the case because this is the one that leaves the physical marks and is also the most obvious. Without being too flippant about this, it is also the picture that is painted by the mass media on this subject; so the typical thought is that there is physical abuse.

If physical abuse and violence is a part of a relationship then it is almost guaranteed that this is only the tip of the iceberg in terms of the level of abuse that is taking place.

The one thing that violence creates in a relationship is one of the most basic fears. That is the fear of being physically hurt, and then ultimately the fear of death. Fear is one of the most basic of human emotions that will start to undermine any self-respect and dignity in a victim. Once fear starts at this level, there is already a degree of control that is present and that will only lead to the other types of abuse that we will talk about next.

Manipulation

Manipulation can take many forms and can occur on many different levels. In fact when it comes down to it, a lot of the other things that we talk about here; are all forms of manipulation. The main problem with manipulation is that it does not have to come in the ways that are discussed here, in other words it does not have to been mean and nasty, in fact it can be the complete opposite, but still achieve the same end – control.

Manipulation is typically made up of little different things; some of which are outright threatening and nasty, and others that do not appear to be like that at all; and generally there is a mixture of both.

One of the things with manipulation is that it is not always obvious to those that are being manipulated, and at times even the manipulator is not aware that it is even going on. It can be so subtle, but extremely powerful, it just sort of creeps up on the victim and before they know it, they are sucked in.

Let me give you an example here to make it a little clearer. A simple example that does not necessarily make you think of manipulation, but it most certainly is – Nagging.

We all know what nagging is; we have all been on both sides of it at some point in our lives. If you think about it, nagging is simply a means of getting your own way. It is designed to wear down the other person so they will do whatever it is that we want them to do. In other words we are manipulating them, by being annoying, so that we get what we want.

Don't get me wrong here, I am not saying that all nagging is abuse, it depends on the amounts and extremes that it is taken to before it gets into the area of abuse, but in terms of simple manipulation, it is most certainly that.

If we take this exact example to an extreme then we are getting into the world of abuse. There is one well known example of this that springs to mind. Have you ever watched 'Keeping up appearances'? Have you ever looked at poor Richard and thought what a poor man, being nagged and manipulated like that all the time. As far as I am concerned what is going on there is very much a form of domestic abuse, although the show does not go into detail of the actual people involved, this man clearly does not have any control over his own life and is essentially used and dominated by his wife. Sounds like abuse to me.

However that is a topic for a little later, for now I just wanted to talk a little about manipulation and what it can do and how it is not always obvious that it is happening. The example that I used here is a very simple and very common one, but the point is that it does take many forms, and when it gets to the point where it is taking away someone's freedom and control over their own lives, then it is most certainly abuse, and without a bruise in sight.

Verbal Abuse

Given the earlier chapter on The Power of Words this one should be a little self-explanatory but there are a few more things that I think that we should take into account here. When using the term verbal abuse I am not just talking about aggressive behaviour or speech with the emotion that goes with it. I am talking about the countless and relentless abuse that usually gets disguised and dismissed. However over time and coupled with the aggression and the out right hostility, these things all add up.

What I am talking about here is the little comments that get thrown in almost constantly. Little things like, 'Did you paint those jeans on? I remember a time when you could wear those jeans without squeezing into them.' In other words, 'You are getting fat.'

Then there are always the comments on the fact that the house is not kept clean, the kids are running riot and so many others, that when added together simply start to eat away at away at the victim's self esteem.

If someone puts you down often enough for long enough then you are eventually going to get worn down. The same applies the other way, in that if someone praises and believes in you often enough for long enough, then you will also believe it. Such is the power of words. In a situation when the abuser has no respect for the victim, you have a situation where the power is used in such a negative way, that the victim really does not stand a chance.

With all of these things put together, soon enough you have an abuser and a victim. The abuser in is in control and the victim is so worn away and effectively down on themselves that not only do they not have the strength to fight back, they do not believe that they have a right to fight back.

Once again there are no bruises, there are no signs, but there is most certainly abuse.

Isolation

One of the things that an abuser will do to help get control over the victim is to isolate them from their friends and family. At the same time you will usually find that the abuser has a full social life and this becomes the only circle of friends that the victim has.

This is another feature of abuse that happens and is not easy to spot as it is going on. It sort of creeps up on the victim and before they know it, they are pretty much alone except for the abuser, the abuser's family and friends.

What this does is create a situation whereby the abuser is effectively surrounded by allies. When the victim does start complaining about the way they are being treated, they have no-one to turn to because all of the people are essentially on the side of the abuser and somehow cannot see the abuser for who they really are. This essentially means that the victim is removed from their support group.

There are lots of different ways that this happens, and more often than not the victim actually thinks they are responsible for removing these people from their lives.

One of the ways in which the isolation becomes self-imposed is by the defensive attitude of the victim. When those outside of the relationship can see what is happening and they try to confront the victim about it, the victim can become defensive of the situation and their partner. Then conflicts begin and the victim decides not to have anything else to do with those people.

Another way isolation is achieved is that the abuser will refuse to get along with the victim's friends. This will create friction and eventually they will then shun anything to do with these friends and therefore will start creating a gap as the victim now becomes stuck in the middle. In order to please their partner the victim takes sides with them and so will therefore have less and less to do with their own friends.

Self imposed isolation also happens because of a sense of shame and embarrassment involved in abuse. Nobody wants to admit that they are a victim, and that they are putting up with a partner who is treating them badly. This is something that can lead a victim to seek self-isolation; especially if friends and families are also putting pressure on them.

You can see how in these simple examples the isolation starts to take shape and also how the victim can be the cause of the isolation, in a round about way.

Manipulation, verbal abuse and isolation start creating a very dim picture for the victim who may not even be aware of what is happening around them.

Financial Dependency

This is just another way the abuser controls the victim. When working with victims one of the things I hear as much as anything else is that they would like to change something, they would like to leave, but they simply cannot afford to do it. The problem is that this can be a very valid point as much as it can be used as an excuse not to deal with the abusive situation.

This is a tool that is used very much by an abuser to maintain control over their victim. By keeping them short of cash and making them financially dependent they are essentially keeping them prisoner. You add this to the isolation, fear and other factors involved in abuse that I have already spoken about and you will get a picture of despair and hopelessness that a victim can find themselves in.

You can often find in this situation that as debt is growing and money is owed that the abuser will usually make sure that all of the debt is in the victim's name. What this means is that the victim does not have any cash, they also have a large amount of debt that is their responsibility to do something about.

In corporate terms financial dependency is called "golden

handcuffs". This means that person who is handcuffed is dependent on the organisation through a financial arrangement and therefore is unable to leave the company because they are essentially handcuffed due to finances. This is no different in a domestic abuse situation in that the victim is held captive by the financial status that they are in, and therefore are unable to leave the relationship, because they simply cannot afford to.

Blackmail

Blackmail is essentially the use of unfair pressure in an attempt to influence someone. Blackmail uses the victim's fear against them. What this means is that blackmail becomes a means of control that uses fear as it base.

This is not so much of the fear of physical abuse; but fear of something negative actually coming true.

A great example of this is when there are children in the relationship; the fear of loosing the children is a powerful example. Essentially the blackmailer creates a situation whereby the victim is afraid to do anything opposed to the abuser for fear of loosing the children.

If you take the fact that the victim has been constantly criticised for their parenting skills, and at same time add this to a threat to take the children away from them, then this becomes a very real fear and means of control.

This is just one example, but there are others that do not need children to be involved. It could be the fear of losing the home, being alone for the rest of their lives, fear for other members in their family and even fear of death. I am sure that you will not be surprised by a statement of something like "If you ever left me, then I will hunt you down and kill you". This is a very powerful statement when you consider that the abuser/victim relationship will be well and truly established and this is something that the victim actually believes could happen.

Blackmail is a tool that is used throughout society, not only in abuse situations. The golden handcuff situation mention earlier is blackmail. Fear is a key factor in any blackmail situation, in that it is the fear of result of actions that will control what the victim will do. Given that fear and control are the corner stone of most abuse situations, then this is a very key tool in the abuser's kit.

Fear (of Physical Abuse)

I am mentioning this one separately because I think it is important enough to do so. Fear of physical abuse does not need abuse to have happened for this to be real. All that is required is the belief by the victim that it could actually happen. Once the victim believes that the abuser is capable of hurting them, and will actually do so, then that fear becomes very real for them.

The problem is that it is as powerful if not more powerful than the actual abuse that may or may not have happened before. The thing with physical abuse, once it actually happens, is that it change a number of things. For one, the victim may actually draw the line at the physical abuse and may do something about it. If the physical abuse does not happen, then the victim is able to justify a lot of things to themselves in terms of not having to take the action in the first place.

This can sound a little confusing, so I will try and explain it a bit more here. Generally speaking a victim will be able to justify a lot of things to themselves, and even to other people who may suggest abuse by saying something like "there has never been any violence; I would not stand for it". Even though the threat of violence is very real and is very controlling, but because it has not happened, it changes the rules in the victim's mind and they are able to convince themselves that it is not really as bad as everyone thinks.

On the other hand, once violence has become part of the

relationship, it takes on a different perspective, not only for the victim, but also for those on the outside, who now have a very strong platform for demonstrating the abuse.

The easiest way to look at this is if a victim were to call the police and say that they were being abused, in that there are a lot of threats of physical abuse, there is manipulation, verbal abuse and all the other things that we have talked about here, what do you think the reaction would be from the police? The police will be sympathetic and will advice taking action, but they will not get involved, because there has not been a crime committed. On the other hand if a victim were to call the police with physical evidence of abuse, it all becomes very serious, very quickly.

This is why the fear of physical abuse is more powerful than the actual abuse itself, because it changes the way things are in terms of perception, justification and many other mental and emotional view points, especially in the victim.

Jealousy

As with a lot of the things discussed in this chapter, jealousy is also in degrees and severity. Jealousy in small doses can be quite flattering in that it means that someone cares enough to be jealous. It also means that there is also some degree of concern that the relationship is not going to last forever and stops the onset of contentment.

On the other hand jealousy in the extreme becomes abuse in that it becomes a prison for the victim because there is also a huge degree of control that is put in place.

In terms of creating isolation it is used to stop contact with anyone who could possibly been seen as a threat to the relationship. The abuser will use manipulation in many forms in order to protect what they have, and jealousy is a main driver.

It can also get to the point where the victim is controlled in how they look and how they dress. In order not to provoke the abuser's jealousy they will make sure that they are not seen as appealing in order to save themselves from the wrath of the abuser.

The trouble with this kind of jealousy is that while the abuser will want to make sure that the victim is looking their best for them. there are also the comments that they are looking too good and too attractive for others. This also adds to the control and isolation.

Infidelity

I am including this here because generally speaking this also forms another aspect of abuse in a relationship. Although this is not seen as abuse I think that it qualifies in that is shows that there is a distinct lack of respect for the other party in the relationship.

When one partner is unfaithful they are not only abusing the other person they are abusing the whole premise of the relationship. This also adds to the abuse because it robs the victim of self-respect and dignity, and also increases the power of the abuser.

Infidelity although not necessarily abuse in and of itself, it does contribute significantly to the whole picture of abuse, and it most certainly says a lot more about how the abuser esteems the victim.

Stripping of self-respect and dignity

In order to gain the levels of control that the abuser is seeking there are two things that need to happen, firstly they need to increase their dominance and secondly and most importantly they need to make sure that the victim is kept down. Stripping the victim of their self-respect and dignity is the best way for them to do this.

When someone does not believe in themselves then they are constantly looking for external validation. I know this all sounds a little bit therapy based, but what I am trying to say is that we all like to try and feel good about ourselves, and there is one thing that will help us do that and that is someone that we look up to telling us that we are great and appreciating us for it.

What this means in real life terms is that the victim will go out of their way to get the approval of the abuser, and that is where a lot of the control comes in.

When a person is put down often enough and long enough they start to believe all of the things that are said about them, and they lose their self-respect and their dignity. The victim can easily be controlled even if very little actual abuse is going on. This is because the victim no longer believes that they deserve better or have enough self worth to fight back. They no longer think about changing the situation, they do not think about leaving, they essentially come to accept their fate, and the state of the relationship.

I suppose you could say that they lose hope. Not only do they lose hope that things will get better, they no longer believe that they should get better. They do not believe that they are worthy of anything more than they have.

Once a victim gets to this point, through whatever means, then it becomes very hard for them to do anything about it. Even if they wanted to, they do not think that they can and they do not think that they should.

It all leads to control

Through this chapter I have been talking about control. That is essentially what an abusive relationship comes down to; the abuser having control over the victim. For an abuser to gain this control they do not have to be physically bigger and stronger, they simply need to be able to dominate the victim and use this dominance to gain complete control. I can not even begin to explain or justify why someone would want to do this and why someone would want to hurt someone that they supposedly love. However I am going to shed a little more light on this issue of control in order to understand this subject better.

From the earliest time and at the most basic level we are told that the biggest and strongest is the one that is in control. If you look at something as simple as a family of apes, it is the biggest and strongest male that is in control of the family. They spend a lot of their time repelling attempts from other males to take their position and gain that control.

Humans are not different and they never have been. All of us, from the earliest age seek control and dominance over our surroundings. Children do it in the playground, they do it at home by rebelling against their parents, and it goes on throughout their lives.

In most cases this desire for control is kept in moderation, but there are times when we all seek more control, even if it is over ourselves and our immediate world. For others it becomes more than that and it almost becomes something that they believe is their right, to be in complete control of their lives. This is where the abuser's mindset develops. They believe that they have the right to be able to control those around them. Not only do they seek control, they think that they should be in control and therefore they are prepared to do whatever they need to do to get it.

As I said I cannot go into all of the details of why abusers do what they do, and I am by no means trying to justify it in any way because I do not believe that it can be justified in any way, what I am trying to do is just make you think a little about control and how it is very much a part of our lives and even our basic makeup.

The way domestic abuse works is that one person is more dominant and controlling while the other is passive. The abuser being more dominant controls the victim. That is how the abuse comes about, and that is what keeps it going. But there is one other aspect of control that I will talk about later and that is that control has to be given as well as taken. Whilst the victim does not mean to do it, they unwittingly contribute to this scenario in some ways. The sort of control we are talking about has to be given as well as taken. It can be given out of fear or for other reasons mentioned here, but it is still given.

Any/ALL of the above

It is important to be aware that all of the things mentioned above can be occurring at the same time. The ultimate aim is control, but the method to get that control can be any combination of the things above and then each of them in different ways and different amounts.

For example someone who is violent is very clearly dominant and therefore will be very overt in the way that they do these things. Someone else could be much more subtle and less overtly dominant therefore the methods that are used are obviously going to be a little different.

It is also important to point out that just because these things are present in a relationship does not mean that there is abuse. Apart from the violence and verbal abuse, the rest are present in all relationships to a certain degree. What I am saying here is that it is not simply because they are present, it is how they are present, and in what amounts they are there that determine when it is abuse, or simply dominant personalities at play. This can be a very grey area, and there are many various factors to take into account. I will talk about this a little more in the next chapter.

WHEN DOES IT BECOME ABUSE?

To be honest with you, this is the third time that I have tried to answer this question. At first glance you think that this would be a fairly straight forward question and one that has a pretty clear answer. That is what I thought when I started writing this chapter two previous times, however each time I discovered that there is more to this question than first meets the eye.

The first time there is violence there is an abusive situation, however if you look at all of the other interplay of factors that go along with abuse, then it becomes a lot more complex to define when abuse begins if there had been no violence or verbal abuse.

When I started to write this chapter the previous times my first thought was that we have an abuse situation when there is a dominant party in the relationship taking away the freedom and options of the victim. Which in a very broad sense is true, however I do not think that this answer actually fully covers this question in all its complexities. A deeper look into this issue reveals that this question raises more and more questions, rather than just provide a simple answer to them. I will give you some of the questions that came to mind and see where we can take it from there.

The first question that came to mind is – "is it abuse if the victim does not feel abused?" When you start thinking about this question you will realise that this is also a lot more complicated than it seems. If you remember back when I was talking about Richard in 'Keeping Up Appearances' I mentioned that this situation in my view was abuse, however as far as Richard was concerned this was just normal, so is he being abused?

It may be that Richard was even happy with his relationship and was therefore happy to be treated like he was. So you have to wonder if it really is abuse, if the victim is happy with it.

But then if you take it a little further, you have to wonder if he is really happy, or has just gotten to the point where he is beaten down and has come to accept it, rather than be happy with it. Surely then if the victim is not happy with it, it then becomes abuse. But again, just because someone is not happy in a relationship, does not mean that they are a victim and they are being abused. Now you should start seeing the fact that this is a much more complex situation than first meets the eyes.

Furthermore what if there is a victim that is in fact being abused, but the abuser is not aware of it? Is this still abuse? But then you have to have a look at the motives behind it all in the first place. If the abuser is not aware of it, as far as they are concerned, they are not doing anything wrong therefore is this still abuse? Must the abuser be aware of what they are doing to create a situation of abuse?

You see what I mean about all of the questions this raises, and I am not finished yet.

So if the victim and the abuser are not aware of it, is it abuse? What if the so called abuser is being so dominant because the victim has taken such a passive role that someone needs to step up and take control?

There are so many different questions and variations that go into making up this one question that I guess it would be almost impossible to answer. Every situation is different and the people involved are different. I guess you could also say that everyone's view on what constitutes abuse is also different for that matter, so it is almost impossible to give a direct and conclusive answer.

What I will suggest is that it becomes abuse when there is no mutual respect and understanding between the parties involved. When one person dominates over everything, regardless of the needs and wants of the other person, and when the victim does not have the freedom to make their own decisions and has no choice but to accept what the other person wants, whether they like it or not, then this is abuse.

I know that is a very broad and sweeping statement that does not answer the question, but I do not think it would be right to give a more specific answer simply because each person and case is different.

WHY DON'T THEY JUST LEAVE?

Until I started to learn about domestic abuse this would have been my first answer to the problem. Why don't they just leave, why do they put up with it?

I could even go so far as to say that I would almost blame the victim for staying and allowing it to happen. On the surface it seems to be the most sensible thing for anyone to do. I mean if they won't leave and won't do something about it, then perhaps they deserve all that they get.

I suppose the same could also be said of the homeless people. I mean there are lots of other options available before they end up on the streets. Surely they make their choices, and therefore where they are is simply their own fault.

But I have become a little wiser than that, and I have to say that when faced with this question now, I can see that there are a myriad of valid and real reasons why they don't just leave. I am going to go into that in more detail in the next section, but I wanted to include this in this section because I think it is important to think about this whole thing in different terms.

If you think about all of the things that we have talked about already in terms of the different kinds of abuse, and then look at the fact that it is ultimately control that the abuser is looking to achieve then you have to realise that the victim does not have a great deal of control over their lives and their situation.

One thing I am very passionate about is empowering the individual to have options and choices. The complete opposite is true of an abuser; they work towards removing options and therefore choices from the victim. At the same time they are focused on destroying the victim mentally and emotionally.

It seems to me that the victims that do manage to get out of an abusive situation deserve some kind of medal or award, because it takes such an extraordinary person to break free of the abuse, the mental and emotional bombardment and finally take themselves back from the abuser's control.

Looking at this a different way may help put this into perspective. For most people going to work each day is simply something they endure, because they have to. Even though at work they are not abused, they are not put down, and do not have every second of their life dictated to them. They are free to leave any time that they want. But for most people they feel they are trapped in what they are doing for any number of reasons. The most prominent reason is that they need to money to support their family and their lifestyle. So as much as they hate it, they turn up each day, simply because they have to.

I use this as an example because I think it shows how people who do not believe they have options behave. They carry on doing things they do not want to do, simply because they do not believe that they have any control over it.

If you take this example and compare it to a domestic abuse situation you can start to appreciate how little choice these victims believe they have. Not only are they not encouraged to think for themselves, they are taught that they cannot think for themselves and the only purpose they really serve on the planet is to be there for the abuser.

Now, do you see how the question - 'why don't they just leave' starts to look quite pitiful when you start thinking about it. If someone who is completely free to make their choices, but do not know that they can, or believe that the choices are too hard or even impossible to make, that they will stay in a situation where they are not happy, imagine what a victim is going through all of the time. Not only are they trapped in the relationship by their own fear, their own lack of self-respect and dignity, they are told over and over again that there is no way out for them.

Sooner or later they are going to believe and sooner or later simply leaving is not even something they are able to even consider.

I guess one main lesson from this chapter is not to be so quick to judge; both on the part of those looking in and those that are victims. Believe me there is no-one that judges a victim for their lack of action etc. more than the victim themselves.

At some point the victim simply looses hope, and then they blame themselves for the situation they are in, but they simply do not know how to get out. That is why they don't just leave.

IGNORANCE AND EXPECTATIONS

One of the things that I want to touch on specifically is that everyone's idea of what to expect from a relationship is different as is their understanding of what rights they have in a relationship.

I talked earlier about the rights in a relationship, but we have to keep in mind when talking about this that the rights that I spoke of earlier come from western law. There are many cultures that have different laws when it comes to the rights in a relationship.

Regardless of where a relationship is based it is the expectations of the people involved that have a huge bearing on what will go on within the relationship. As well as the expectations of the culture and different religions of the individuals who have come from many different walks of life involved, their past experiences also come into play and determine the expectations in the current relationship.

For example it is often said that someone who was raised in an abusive household will often go on to be an abuser. The same is also said of a victim. If someone has been a victim in a previous relationship it is not uncommon for them to become a victim again.

I do not think that I need to quote statistics and facts to make the point here. The point is that the expectations and idea of what a relationship should be will also play a major part in how a relationship is going to develop.

Essentially the thing with expectations and people is that we all like to live up to the expectations that are placed on us. Not only those that are placed on us by others, but also the one we place on ourselves. We do not like to be proven wrong, so we do all that we can to live up to our own expectations.

The same can be said for those people that we look up to and those people who have influence over us. We want to deliver what they expect of us and so we do what we can to make sure that is what we do. The abuser also has expectations which do not come across as request but as demands. They will come in the form of "I expect you to..."

In this way the expectation has been placed on the victim, and the victim will try and live up to that expectation.

This is something that happens without the victim realising, as far as they can see they are simply doing what is expected of them, and so they do not notice how controlling the situation has become.

This is another complexity that is thrown into the mix of what relationships are and how they are going to pan out in the future. Ignorance and expectations play a big part in the relationship, and it can also be very much a basis for an abusive relationship.

HOW DOES IT HAPPEN IN THE FIRST PLACE?

There are so many different factors at play here that once again it is not a simple question to answer. When you are dealing with people and different situations it is impossible to offer a blanket statement that is going to be right in even a small number of cases. You have to think back to the beginning of this book when I spoke about this being a book that is intended to provoke thought and provide some insight, rather than solve all your problems.

I believe that the information that you have read so far will have already started you thinking about the situation in greater depth and hopefully you are gaining a lot more insight on this matter than perhaps you had in the past. That is the purpose of this book, to get you thinking, once you are thinking and getting a different view on things, then you are able to think about options and changes a little more. That is what my job is here; to provoke thought. That is what this chapter is designed to do, provide some insight, but ultimately you need to look at the individual situation and find the answers, I can't give them to you from here. I will give you some guidance here, but not answers.

With any abusive relationship there are, for the purposes of this book anyway, two people involved. Obviously there needs to be an abuser and a victim. The question is which one came first and which one created the other. Now this may sound confusing and you may be wondering what I am talking about. Well it is simple and complicated at the same time, and I will try and explain it a little more.

Let's assume to start with that when the relationship began, it was not abusive. Abuse generally sets in gradually over time rather than instantly. When two people come into a relationship they do not come with a clean slate, they come with their baggage. There is a whole life of experience and there are their individual personalities, habits, preconceptions of a number of different things, one of those being the role they are going to play in the relationship.

So what we have in the beginning is two people who have been shaped and moulded by a number of things and they will bring all of that into the relationship. There are a number of different combinations that will come out of the merging of two different people. Something that can also emerge from this relationship is an abuser and a victim.

The dominant personality will start ruling and will ultimately become the abuser and the less dominant personality will ultimately become the victim. Which is generally true, however it can work a little differently, in that perhaps the less dominant personality, by the fact that they are far less dominant can create the dominant position for the other person.

If you have someone who is very timid and very shy and lacking in self-confidence in the beginning what they tend to do is to defer everything to the other person. They do not make any decisions and they do not do anything without seeking the consent of the other person. Over time the other person has to assume the dominant role, just to simply offset the extremes of the other person. Over time this can lead to an abusive situation because once this kind of thing starts, it will continue to progress.

On the other hand you have someone who is very dominant and comes into the relationship with the idea that they are in fact in control and will then continue with this mode until they have the control they believe they deserve, and therefore creating the victim on the other side.

What it comes down to is that for a relationship to work there needs to be balance. Ideally it will be balanced by two people who are even and level, and therefore the relationship is stable.

If one party is not balanced, so to speak, then the other person has to change to create the balance in order for things to work. If one person starts out deferring to the other and essentially forcing the other into the dominant role, in order to maintain the balance; this can lead to the situation whereby the abuser has been almost created by the victim.

On the other side, if one takes the dominant position, it essentially forces the other into the passive side, to provide the balance. This is where the abuser creates the victim.

Obviously there are many other factors that are involved in this. The personalities of the people involved and a whole range of other factors will come into play and determine how far this is taken, but there will be balance, one way or another.

If you look at a relationship where there are two dominant people, and wonder how they ever manage to make it work, it is because even though they are both dominant, there is still balance. It may be a fiery relationship, but there is balance. You will find that there will still be an offset and there will be one who is more dominant than the other.

It may be that there are two very passive people, but there is still balance. Once again, there will still be one dominant person in the relationship.

When we look at the example of Richard in "Keeping Up Appearances" it is clear to see that even though there is one dominant and one passive person involved, it is still balanced, because of that. Richard is obviously a passive personality, and therefore the dominance of his wife offsets that, and that is why the relationship works. I still can't help but think that it is still abuse, but maybe that is just me. As I said, it is not easy to define this.

It does not really matter at the end of the day how the situation started, it is still abuse and it is simply not right. I am not interested in playing the blame game; I am only interested in trying to help provide some understanding that I hope will lead to a solution. Regardless of how it started, there is no situation where someone has a right to abuse another person.

Abuse in a relationship is a gradual thing. There are signs all along the way, that in hindsight seem pretty obvious, but at the time when you are living in it, they are all things that get dismissed along the way. When there is violence involved then the signs are very obvious, even at the time, but we will talk more on this later.

When we go back to the beginning of this chapter and think about it, and how it happens in the first place, it is not an easy answer, there are many factors in place, and I have touched on a few so far. There are so many more, and then on top of that you will get the reasons from the victim, and the reasons from the abuser, and the reasons from the outsiders.

I think in terms of this book, the safest thing to say is that even if there is suspicion a relationship may be heading in the direction of abuse; then do everything you can to remedy the situation, before it is too late.

As abuse is generally a gradual thing, and tends to increase over time, it must be that the people involved are not happy. It does not have to hit the extremes for the people involved to be unhappy.

One of the things that we will talk about in more detail later is why people stay in an unhappy and abusive relationship. Once it does get to a certain point there are not a lot of options left for the victim, as far as they know, however before then there are many reasons why people stay. The same as there are many reasons someone believes that they have a right to be abusive to their partner.

It is not a simple thing, and I am sure there are as many theories about the whole thing that are complete opposite to each other that it is almost impossible for anyone to give reasons for abuse without getting the specific details of the individuals involved.

I do hope that this chapter has given you a little more insight into relationships, and perhaps you are able to apply it to a situation that you are aware of and perhaps you can use some of the insights that you now have to make a difference.

WHERE IS THE CONTROL?

In the previous chapter we have spoken about what abuse is and how it happens. We also tried to answer the question of when does it become abuse and discovered that it is not an easy question to answer.

This chapter is about looking at what is going on within a relationship and seeing where it all sits. It is about taking the time to look at the relationship and trying to build a sort of map and then decide if this is what you would call an acceptable pattern for a good relationship.

Generally speaking there is a dominant person in a relationship, even when the relationship is built on an equal footing; this is the person who will take the lead when required. On the other hand it could be that there is a very dominant person in the relationship and all of the control is there. Once you have decided where the control is there are a series of questions that you can ask yourself that will help you to evaluate the relationship.

- Does the person with the control use it responsibly?
- Do they take into account the wishes of the other person in the relationship?
- Do they try and share the responsibility with their partner?
- Do they believe they have a right to the control?
- Do they seek to gain more control?
- Is the less controlling person happy with their position?

The tone and direction of these questions should give more insight into this issue and will act as a point of reference to look at the relationship and see what is going on.

We have seen that it is difficult to define absolutely or pin point when abuse begins in a relationship therefore we have to look at the way the relationship is laid out and where it is going. That is how we can determine if we have an abusive relationship brewing, or if it is OK the way it is.

The point of this chapter is to give you a little prod not just to take it for granted that these things are happening, but just take a few minutes to look around you and evaluate what is going on.

WHAT IS TOLERATED IS VALIDATED

Abuse is something that is gradual; there are several things that happen along the way that create an abusive relationship. One of the things that fuels abuse is the fact that the victim remains in the relationship even when things start to get out of balance. By staying in the relationship, they are saying that the abuse is acceptable. Unless abuse is nipped in the bud at the onset it will continue and not only will it continue it will escalate.

The thing with putting up with something, once or even twice is that even though you may not like it, it is going to keep happening. Let us take an example of the first time there is violence.

The first time violence is used by the abuser, there is obviously going to be a lot of things that will happen. Firstly, once the victim recovers from the shock etc. they will more than likely confront the abuser about it, and let them know that is simply not acceptable, how dare they and all those kind of things. Chances are the abuser will be apologetic, promise that it will never happen again and so forth. The victim will usually agree that it will never happen again and then let it go. After all the victim obviously loves the abuser and they do not want the relationship to end. For that matter the abuser must love the victim and more than likely believes all the things they said.

All that is fine the way that it is; and it may be just a one off. But when it happens the next time, what is the story then?

This time is a little different; the victim still goes through all the usual stuff, probably even starts to leave. The abuser is really apologetic, begs them to stay. All that sort of thing; and the victim will give in this one last time.

Then the third time, this time when the victim confronts the abuser they are not so apologetic. This time they are even more aggressive about it, blaming the victim for making them angry etc. Probably by now they are even becoming more threatening and the victim is now afraid. A pattern has developed whereby the abuser gets angry, the victim gets beat up. If there is talk of leaving by the victim, instead of begging and apologies there are now threats. They are now believed, because the abuser has now shown what they can, and will do. Now there is a full abusive relationship with the abuser getting stronger and the victim getting weaker. And the balance is maintained.

This is just one example, and to be honest it is the easiest one to use because violence is easily defined. Some of the other types of abuse we have discussed are more subtle and more gradual, and can in fact take over before anyone can see it.

But the point of the example is that the first two times it was tolerated, OK there was a point made after each one, and even a threat to leave, but if the victim stayed in this environment, for whatever reason, they are allowing the abuse to continue. They may think that they did not stand for it, but in essence they did. At the end of it, it was something that was tolerated, and therefore the abuser knows that they can get away with it, and has been demonstrated on the previous two occasions, so it is going to continue.

Now the point of tolerating being mistreated is not simply confined to violence, it essentially runs across our entire lives. In fact it is not even confined to domestic abuse, the whole issue of tolerating and therefore validating is something that affects all of us all of the time.

It is easy for me to sit here and talk about this, I do not live your life and I do not live in an abusive relationship, and I am aware of that. What I am trying to say here is that if you let people treat you a certain way, then they will think that they can do that all the time and they will keep doing it.

At some point in an abusive relationship the victim has got to realise that this relationship is not the one that they had in mind when they started on it, that is the time to do something about it. Once again it comes down to options and choices. People think they are in a relationship and have made commitment etc.

but if their lives or well being is at risk then they don't have to stay in that relationship.

If you are not getting treated with respect and equality, then do something about it. Every time it happens and every time you do nothing about it, for whatever reason you are saying that it is OK to treat you like that. You do not have to endorse it; you simply have to tolerate it in one way or another.

By saying nothing or at the very least doing nothing, you are saying that you are not going to do anything about it because it is OK. The longer you make it OK, the harder it is to change it. I know there are lots and lots of reasons to stay and not to leave, and we are going to talk about them. But please keep in mind that you what is tolerated is validated; regardless of the reason or excuses.

This does not only apply to those in domestic abuse situations, it applies to all people everywhere. If your boss is not treating you with respect, then change your job, if you spouse is not treating you in the way that you want to be treated, find a solution to the problem don't just endure it. Life is too short to get stuck in situations that make you unhappy.

Please take this one on board, if you get nothing else from this book, you do have options and you do make your choices, please do not put up with an unhappy existence, things can change if you choose to work at it. There are always alternatives, always.

POWER HAS TO BE GIVEN AS WELL AS TAKEN

Control and power are pretty much the same thing in this context and the point I want to emphasise here is that in order for the abuser to gain the control that they have, the victim also has to give them that control.

This may also come across as blaming the victim, but that is not what it is about. I am working on the premise that it is not only people in abusive relationships that will read this book. It could be anyone, it could even be someone who may be heading down that path, this information might therefore help those who are not in abusive relationships by helping to prevent it before it starts and who knows it may just save someone's life.

This chapter as with the previous one it not just confined to domestic abuse, it covers all of our lives. Just like people will treat us as badly as we allow them to, it also goes that they can only gain control over us, if we allow them to. Again I am talking generally here, and I am sure there are many instances where someone could say that it is not true, but generally speaking it is true. The same as it is in a domestic abuse situation. At the same time the abuser is working to take control from the victim, the victim is also to an extent surrendering that control to the abuser.

I know that there are many reasons for this involved, but the point is, when the abuser controls the victim, through whatever means, the victim has somehow surrendered that control somewhere along the way.

When we look at the same example as in the previous chapter, once the victim decides to give in to the threats in the third instance of the violence, without doing something about it, but agreeing to stay in a violent relationship, (albeit out of fear), then they are surrendering control to the abuser.

The thing about it is, even if is a gradual thing, without the violence, once the control has been given it is very hard to get back. Once someone has power there is one thing that they do not want, and that is to loose that power.

When someone starts to dictate to someone else how they should live their life, how they should dress, who they can and can't talk to and all the other things that we talked about, then they are gaining control, a little at a time, but getting the power nonetheless.

Each time we allow someone to tell us what to do; then we are giving them the power. It happens all the time, and most of the time we do not realise that it is.

An abuser has the power over the victim because it has been given, or surrendered along the way.

This follows directly from the previous chapter about tolerating and validating. When you let things slide by without doing something about it, you are saying that it is OK. The same works when you allow someone to start controlling you, when you do not stop it, it just sort of continues by default. When there is no violence the power shift is gradual, but never ending, unless it is nipped in the bud from the beginning.

One of the things I will talk about later is how to get this power back. The important thing I want to emphasise is not getting power over the abuser, but it is about getting the power back on the inside of the victim. That is where the true power lies. It is that power that needs to be awakened in order for the victim to escape.

THE CONVEYER BELT

Here I want to talk about an important issue that follows on from the previous two chapters. It is how we end up in whatever situation we find ourselves in life. I understand that a victim will often blame themselves for their situation, and it is likely that even abusers also sometimes wonder how their lives have worked out the way it has. This situation is also applicable to most people. Most people never really stop to think about it, they just wonder how their life has worked out the way that it has.

I am no exception in this respect. A few years ago I actually underwent the exercise of looking at my life and realising that this is not want I wanted when I set out on this journey. At that point I was able to change some things about myself and start on a different path. It was not easy to do and there are many things that I had to leave behind along the way, but it is an exercise that I went through and continue to go through.

The point is that life has a habit of just sort of leading us on, without us realising what is happening, and without us taking the time to think about where we are going and what we are doing. I think this is an important thing to understand especially in the context of domestic abuse.

When a relationship starts out, there is no victim and there is no abuser. What you have is two people that like each other and want to spend time with each other.

The next stage that will follow will be that the people will fall in love and then there will be talk of some kind of future together. From there on it is likely that they live together, married or not, perhaps have kids and then the daily grind called life sets in.

At some stage through all this, the relationship will start to change, and this is the same for everyone, the infatuation sort of disappears and a level of comfort sets in. It is rare that the infatuation will continue indefinitely, and more often than not the day to day overtakes just about everything else.

It is once the infatuation and courtship finishes that the abuse starts. Keeping in mind that it is not always physical, but at some stage the dominant personality starts to emerge and the victim is also created. Left unchecked this continues until there is an abusive relationship in full swing.

The point that I am trying to make with this chapter is that it is almost like we are on a conveyer belt that is moving us in a direction, and we just sort of get carried along with it, because that is the way it goes. It is rare that someone will step off the Conveyer Belt and change direction. It can happen in many small ways, but in terms of a complete life change, it does not happen often.

This is another reason why I am writing this book, because it draws attention to what is going on. Once you understand what is happening, it is easier to think about it and then do something about it. Too often we just live our lives without ever taking the time to think about what is going on or even if we are happy with what is going on.

I am sure there are many people who once they sit back and think about it, they are less than happy with the way things have turned out for them.

Try this little exercise for a minute. Think back to when you were a teenager, and you were dreaming of the future and all the things you would like to do and what sort of life you would like to be living when you are older. Now compare this to how your life is now. I am sure you will find that there are not many things in common between the two. Sure when we were teenagers, we dreamed of all sorts of things, most of them are never going to happen, but even so, they were things that we really wanted.

Now if I was to ask you to pin point the exact moment that it changed and the things you dreamed about were never going to happen and you had to resign yourself to the life you now have; you will find it impossible to do. This is because there is no one single moment, it just sort of happened gradually, almost automatically. That is the point that I am making here, many things just sort of happen, and before we know it, here we are, in 'the land of the unexpected'.

I have a lot more to say about all this, but for this book I just wanted to make you aware of this. It does help to explain how someone can find themselves in a domestic abuse situation, and many other situations, without even realising it.

Life is like a Conveyer Belt, and unless you realise this and make a conscious effort to get off the Conveyer Belt then you are going to find yourself just sort moving along with it, wherever it may be taking you.

BEHIND CLOSED DOORS

I am going to finish this first section by talking about domestic abuse and how no-one knows what goes on behind closed doors. We may think that we know, and we may well in fact have a good idea, but when it comes down to it, no-one knows what goes on behind the closed doors in someone else's house and life.

The reason this book is written in an open and general manner is because it is impossible for me to know the details of other people's lives. I may write it as though I am some kind of expert on this, but the truth is I am working on a general view, and I do not know all of the details. The same applies if you are watching someone in an abusive relationship, unless you live with them, you will not get the whole picture of what is going on and all of the emotions etc. that go along with it.

The other thing that is really a big unknown apart from what goes on is the people that are involved. Are there not many people we know who turn out to be very different from what we expected?

What I am trying to suggest here is that it is not often that we really know a person. We know the image they portray, we know the things that they do in public and what they say, but we do not know what is going on in their minds and we do not know the things that they do not want us to know.

I am going to talk once again about "Keeping Up Appearances" to help explain this. On the outside, the side that we see is that poor Richard is constantly bombarded by his wife; he is brow beaten and manipulated and does not do or say anything about it. The thing that we don't know is why he does it, is he happy or is he simply resigned to the way things are?

We also do not have any of the history, we don't see what else goes on when we are not there watching, we do not know where they both came from, what their upbringing was like, and a whole range of other things that go into making up the relationship.

The same applies to those people whom we think we know. We may even be related to them, but still we only know what they want to tell us and what we are able to figure out for ourselves.

I can give you a great example of this. At the beginning of the book you will have read a bit about Ange and her story. Obviously her ex-husband was convicted by a jury based on the evidence, but there are still many of his friends who think he was the victim in all of this. They find it almost impossible to believe that he was like that at all. For most people outside of the relationship he was funny and charming and witty and all the rest of it. He would talk about how much he loves his kids and his wife and how much he does for them. Then he would get home and treat them all like dirt. Not provide for them, not feed them or clothe them and so on.

This is exactly what I am talking about; nobody knows what goes on behind closed doors. The point that I am making here is that it is not safe to assume that you know what the full story is, and at times you need to be aware that people only show us what they want us to see.

END OF SECTION

So now we have come to the end of the first section. In this section we talked about the different kinds of abuse and covered in detail how you don't need bruises to be abused. We also talked about all the many other things going on in the background of an abusive relationship.

We have talked about how relationships operate or work on a kind of balance, when one partner is extreme, the other person will be extreme in the other direction, in order to maintain that balance.

We have tried to understand a little more about what abuse is, and what it isn't, although this is not very easy to define as there are so many variables to the whole picture.

We also talked a lot about how the major thing in an abusive relationship is control. How this control is taken and kept constitutes the abuse. The trouble with someone having control over someone else is that the victim does not know where to go, or even believe they have the options available to do anything about it.

In the next section we are going to be looking at all this from the victim's point of view. We are going to discuss what goes on apart from just the abuse and the effects that it has on the victim that go far beyond what we see on the surface, and how they eventually get worn out.

I hope that you have started to think a little more about domestic abuse and how it is far more complex than it seems on the surface and I hope that you can see how it can affect people at so many different levels.

THE VICTIM

*I*f you are not a victim of domestic abuse then it is likely that this section will be very surprising to you. If you are a victim then I am sure that much of it will still come as a surprise, but it will make sense. It may even feel like someone just switched on a light bulb on the inside of you. That is ultimately the aim of this section; to bring understanding and light into this gloomy topic.

The idea is that once we can understand what is going on at the different levels, then we are able to do something about it. If you are the victim it should give you some more insight into what is really happening, and then you will be in a position to start changing things, mostly about yourself in the short term, but ultimately about the whole situation.

For those that are reading this because they want to help someone that is in an abusive relationship, this provides some idea of what is going on and therefore more understanding of where things are and how they can help.

The whole point of this section is to provide information. Once you have the information then it is up to you to do what you can with it. With understanding comes a number of things, most importantly is that at least you are thinking about what is going on. Once you are aware of what is going on and thinking about it, then you are able to do a lot more about it.

As we have noted, it is not simply a matter of leaving or staying, there are many reasons why the victim will do what they do and will go through what they go through in order to survive what is happening to them. The ultimate plan is to change the abusive situation or break free of the relationship, but let's start with the information, then work on from there.

I have not been a victim of domestic abuse in the past, and to be honest that is something that I wish to maintain. I can only imagine what it would be like to be treated like that in your own home. The one place in the world that is supposed to be a safe haven, a place where, regardless of what is going on in the outside world, that is the place we can turn to, to get away form it all.

I believe that anyone who is a victim and manages to come out of this situation, and then carry on with the rest of their lives must be applauded because this is a demonstration of how resilient the human spirit is, and how above and beyond everything else we are survivors. It also proves that whilst we are still alive there is always a chance that things can change and things can get better.

What I am trying to say is that there is always hope. As long as you continue to draw breath, there is hope and there is a way to break out of the cycle that you are in, so hang in there, don't let it beat you down, there are better things in this life for you, and it will come.

DENIAL, HOPE AND EXCUSES

There are many things going on with a victim in a domestic abuse situation, and the first thing you may ask is how they let things get so bad. It is easy to understand that at some point down the track they lose their dignity and self-respect, and they can become afraid of the abuser, but surely if this thing happens over time, there must be a point where they can see what is happening and do something about it.

This is a very easy thing to say when you are on the outside looking in, and I am sure that the victim themselves will think back and perhaps ask the same thing at some point, but there is more to it than that. At the earlier stages of abuse there is a lot of denial, hope and excuses. It is when these things can no longer be justified that the victim finds themselves stuck, but in the early stages these are the things that the victim uses to almost defend the abuse going on.

We are going to have a look at these individually, but it is important to understand that these things are generally all happening at the same time and overlapping. They are not used in isolation, although as things progress each one is more prominent that the other. The first stage is denial.

Denial

When we choose a partner, we want to be proud of them and we want to be able to show them off almost as a trophy. This may sound a little strange, but it is true; the same way we like to show off our kids, and our new car. I understand that we are talking about people, but when we have a partner we want to be able to say to others, look how good my partner is and look at how wonderful they are and look at all the good things they have done for me. It is human nature; we like to show off what we have.

Having said that, it does go a lot deeper; we almost feel a need to be proud of our choice of a partner. What this means is that when things are not all sweetness and light, we can dismiss all the bad things, and hang on to the good things.

I am sure we have all heard that love is blind, and to a certain degree that is true. I don't think it is the fact that we do not see the bad points; we do not want to see the bad points, so we deny that they are there.

This even extends to the point where a victim will deny being abused, simply because they do not want to admit that it is happening. This is not just denying it to others outside of the relationship; it is also denying it to themselves.

To admit that they are being abused will mean that they then need to admit that they are not a very good judge of character, that the person that they are in love with is not a good person as well as all of the others things that reflect back at them for making the wrong choice.

Even when there is violence involved in the first two or three instances the victim is able to deny it and dismiss it as something that happened once; that is why they stay there after it happens. It is easier to deny the problem than to face it.

If you are trying to help someone whom you believe to be in an abusive relationship and they are still in the denial phase then it is almost impossible to get through to them. If you persist is trying to make them see what is happening, then as far as they are concerned you are attacking their partner, and therefore attacking them. This is a time to be very careful about how to proceed. If you do keep pushing then you will simply push them away. Chances are the abuser is trying to create the isolation by now, and so it will not take a lot to put a huge gap between you and someone you are trying to help. It is not always a case of denying it to you, they are still denying it to themselves, and there is no way that you will convince them differently at this stage. Be a friend, be supportive, but do not push too hard.

In the early stages this is the real issue, if you don't recognise it as a big problem that needs to be dealt with, then in your mind it will sort of go away, and you will see it as just a passing phase, and gradually you get into the area of hope.

Hope

As there are many parts and many levels to a relationship so also there are many hopes that get wrapped up in the relationship and a lot of them come into play here. The first thing that a victim hopes for once they are able to admit that they do have a problem is that it will change. Hope is very closely coupled with excuses in that it helps them to justify what is happening. We will talk more about excuses in a minute, but for now the victim just hopes that what is going on is a passing phase and that when things change it will all get better.

You have to keep in mind that when we go into a relationship there are also a lot of hopes and dreams that are wrapped up in it in the first place. These hopes are still there, even if it is many years after the start of the relationship, there is always that hope that things will turn out the way that we dreamed they were going to in the beginning.

It is during the earlier stages of the abuse that the victim will be thinking that there are lot of reasons why their partner is behaving like this, and will be hoping that if they can change these reasons then they will be able to change what is happening.

The hope also comes from the abuser in many cases also. When a victim confronts the abuser about what has been going on, the abuser will admit that there is a problem, will apologise and will often promise to change. It is more than likely that they do mean to change, and will change. But usually this will only last for a short time.

In the beginning it is during these times that the victims hope is rekindled and they are able to rebuild all of the hopes for the relationship during these times. However it often only lasts for a short time, perhaps a couple of weeks and maybe even a couple of months.

The thing with these times is that they get fewer and fewer and they gradually last for a shorter time. The reason that they get fewer is that in the earlier times the victim is still clinging to the hope and they use this to give them the strength and courage to confront the abuser about what has been happening. After a while the victim starts losing the hope that things will change and also stops trying to change things. This is when the pure survival mode sets in.

One of the biggest excuses that will come is that they still love the abuser. There are many victims that will refuse to do anything about it because they believe that they still love the abuser. Well that is the excuse that they give anyway.

What I think this is really saying is that they are saying they still love the person that they fell in love with before they became the abuser. This is where hope also plays a part in that they are still clinging onto when the relationship was good, and they did want to be with that person, and so they still try and believe that it can be like that again and that it will get better.

The thing with hope and the excuses is that it is difficult to determine at want point the victim stops believing them. It gets to the point where they have given up hope that things are going to change, but then they try to excuse the fact that they no longer have any hope, which is essentially admitting the failure. This is to themselves, not so much to the outside world. What happens then is that they start to hope that the excuses they are making are true.

What this means is that they no longer have the hope in the relationship, so they start to hope that the excuses that they are making are going to be true. It all helps in the justification of the fact that the relationship has essentially failed.

Essentially it is with hope and excuses that the victim clings onto the relationship as they want it to be. A relationship is a major part of a person's life and it is not something that they want to give up on easily. They will do all that they can to hang on to even the tiniest spark in order to keep the hope alive, and therefore keep the relationship alive.

It is during the denial and the hope stages that the excuses are really evident because it does provide the justifications for what is happening.

Excuses

Excuses are the things that we as people use throughout our lives in order to protect ourselves and our loved ones from the reality of the world and our own shortcomings.

We all do it, all the time. It is a natural reaction to make excuses for the way that things are and how things have turned out for us. The worse the situation we find ourselves in, the more excuses we will make to cover for it. It is human nature to do this and when someone is a victim and even an abuser in a domestic abuse situation the excuses are there to help justify the whole thing.

During the denial stage, there are many excuses, but they are made more to themselves in order to justify what is going on so as to hide the fact that the problem exists in the first place.

During the hope stage the excuses are used to diminish what is really going on, and also to excuse the abuser for what they are doing. Once this stage starts to wear off it does not mean that the excuses will.

What changes throughout these stages is that the victim still believes, or at least really tries to believe the excuses in order to keep the dream alive. After these two stages the excuses are essentially used for the benefit of others, on the outside.

After the denial and then the hope have faded there is still very much an element of saving face and not admitting to others that there is a real problem. Nobody wants to admit that the person that they fell in love with and chosen to be with turned out to be someone who abuses them. Admitting that means admitting to being a big failure.

The whole point of excuses is to protect ourselves from admitting that we are not perfect and that we have made bad choices, mistakes etc. So it is natural that a victim will not want this to be known to everyone and will therefore go to great lengths to cover it up.

Summary

Although I can sit here and write about these things and define them in clear cut stages, the human mind is not nearly as simple as that, and neither is a relationship. I have written it this way for clarity however there are many things going on at the same time, many things overlap and the complexities are much more detailed that can be put on paper.

The point of highlighting these three things is that they do happen in the mind of the victim, although they are often not aware of it, and that is one of the key things I want to emphasise here. They are not aware of it.

If a victim was aware of what was actually happening then perhaps it would be a little different for them, and they may actually do something about it in the earlier stages. Perhaps not, chances are that if they were aware of it, they would still be determined to hang on to the idea of the ideal relationship as it was in the beginning and the information that is contained here would become part of the denial process, in that it would become something like "that is not happening to me, because I do not have a problem in my relationship".

You can see how complex this all becomes, and how a relationship will continue past the early stages of abuse. By the time the denial and hope have passed, the abuse is now deeply ingrained. That is essentially how it unfolds and how it grows to a stage where it is out of the control of the victim. All the time these stages are going on, the abuser is gaining power over the victim and taking more and more control all of the time. There is no respite from the abuser.

There is also no respite from the day to day life of the victim either. Being a victim in a domestic abuse relationship is just one part of their life. At the same time they still have to get on with everything else that is part of their lives.

For most of us the pressures of day to day life is enough to wear us out and keep us busy. Add to that the fact that a victim is also being abused, manipulated and controlled; they almost do not have time for much else. That includes the time it takes to evaluate what is going on around them and see what is happening to them.

It just becomes part of the daily grind, and so it just sort of continues.

The other point to consider here is also that the abuser is more than likely blaming the victim for what is happening at the same time. The victim is also feeling responsible for letting the abuser down and creating this. We are going to look at this in the next chapter when we play 'The Blame Game'.

THE BLAME GAME

Astonishing at it may seem it is quite often that the victim feels responsible for what is going on. This is another big reason why they stay through the early stages; because they feel responsible for the relationship failing and so they try and do what they can to fix it.

Unfortunately this is not something that is in their power to do, as it is the abuser that is the cause of the problem and not the victim. It is the abuser that brings the abuse, not the victim; however the abuser will be painting a very different story to the victim. The abuser will be using a tool called 'The Blame Game'.

Basically, The Blame Game is where we as people in order not to accept responsibilities for things that we do or have done shift the blame for the problem onto someone or something else.

In the case of domestic abuse it is no different for the abuser. They will tell the victim over and over again how it is their fault that the abuser feels the need to do what they do. This is even true in the situations where there is violence. The abuser will tell the victim that they make them so angry that they lash out. They will tell the victim that it is because of the things that they do and say that create the problem in the first place.

It is the same for the other kinds of abuse also. When they are verbally abusing and putting the victim down it will be because the victim is a bad parent, putting on weight, being stupid and all of those things.

When it comes to the isolation it will be because the victim has friends and family who don't like the abuser, and they are the ones that are causing the problems.

You can see how this works by now. Essentially the abuser makes the victim believe that it is their fault that they are getting treated that way because they deserve it because they are not doing the right things, living the right way, talking to the right people. All this is of course the way that the abuser wants things to be.

The victim starts to believe all of the things that the abuser is telling them. Not only are they doing all the wrong things that the abuser is accusing them of, they are also failing as a partner in the relationship because they are obviously not able to keep their partner happy.

You have to keep in mind that whilst the abuser grows stronger the victim grows weaker and the constant attacks and the laying of the blame starts to take root and become as much a part of the abuse as anything else.

It is not uncommon for a victim to believe they are responsible for any act committed against them. Even in the case of rape by a stranger the victim can feel that they created the situation, and that is also encouraged by the abuser. Imagine if that same sentiment was told to the victim day after day, they really take on that responsibility.

As the abuse gets worse, and it generally always will, so the blame will also continue. It will get the point where the abuser will be blaming the victim for ruining their life and blaming them for all of their failures. This is the same as making excuses, and the abuser needs to make excuses for their own failures the same as anyone does. The problem is they do not just make excuses; they put all of the pressure on the victim.

So now what you have is a victim who not only has to defend their situation to the outside world, they have to defend it to themselves, because they do start believing that they are in fact to blame for it.

What this means is that the victim does not see themselves as a victim, they see themselves as getting what they deserve because they have created this awful relationship and they have failed in what they wanted to do.

This just becomes one more thing that takes away the self-respect and dignity from the victim and when you start adding all of the things together you can start to see why there is not a simple solution and also how far the abuse actually goes. It is only when you really start to look below the surface that it starts to show how bad things are for the victim, and you can start to understand how they will ultimately become resigned to what is going on and stop fighting.

In the next chapter we are going to talk a little more about relationships and try to understand some more reasons why they stay in a relationship that is so obviously not working and not healthy. A relationship that essentially sucks away at their mind and their emotions until there is not a lot left.

FEAR, FEAR AND MORE FEAR

We have spoken quite extensively about how the abuser seeks to control the victim. One of the ways, and perhaps the most significant way that an abuser does this is by using fear.

I am not talking just about the fear of physical abuse, it goes much further than that. Fear is perhaps one of the strongest emotions that people have. It will drive people to do extraordinary things that will go far above and beyond anything they could have imagined.

I am going to talk about some of the fears that the victim develops and how powerful they are when it comes to controlling them. Before I do that though, I want to talk about fear in general and hopefully give you a deeper insight into the nature of fear.

Whilst it is true that fear is a very powerful emotion, generally speaking it is also a very negative emotion. There are times when fear can be used positively, but generally speaking it is used as a tool to prevent someone doing something, that they otherwise would.

The thing with fear is that it is not generally based on rational thinking. I was told a long time ago that if you break the word fear into an acronym what you end up with is False Evidence Appearing Real. What this is saying is that generally speaking the thing that you are afraid is not necessarily real, although it seems very real at the time, if you apply reason and logic to it, there generally is nothing to fear.

There are ways of dealing with fear that I will talk a little more about in a later section, but for now I do want to try and make the point that fear does not need to have a strong foundation and basis to be powerful enough to control a person. In fact it is generally the opposite that is true, fear is not usually grounded on truth and reality, but that does not make it any less powerful.

Let me give you an example of what I am talking about here. I am afraid of heights. I try to overcome this fear and generally do not let it get in the way of something that I want to do; however it does not stop me feeling nervous and uptight when I am in a high place.

I know that when I am in a high place I am safe. I am not talking about hanging on the top of a flag pole or anything like that; I am talking about being up high in a building, or on a Ferris wheel or something like that. These are safe places to be. There is no chance of me falling or anything like that; nonetheless my natural reaction is to stay away from high places. Reason and logic tells me there is nothing to be afraid of, but the fear is there nonetheless.

This is a very simple example, and I am sure that it is one that a lot of people can relate to. The point is that the fear is not based on anything that is real. In that it is not based on something that is likely to happen, but it is there nonetheless.

Fear is a very powerful emotion, and whether it is based on something real or not, the fear itself is very real. It is the fear that is the real driver not the object of fear. So with that in mind I want to look at some of the things that a victim in a domestic abuse relationship are afraid of, and how a lot of the time the abuser either creates the fear or uses it as much as a weapon as all of the other things that we have previously spoken about.

Fear of Danger from Abuser

Firstly and most obviously there is the fear of physical abuse and pain from the abuser. This does not just apply to someone who is or has been physically abused, it applies to anyone in an abusive relationship who believes that their abuser can and will hurt them physically.

That is a very important point that you need to keep in mind here. There does not need to be violence for the victim to be afraid that there can be. They only need to believe that it can happen. In fact the fear of physical abuse is probably more of a factor for someone who has not been physically abused than it is for someone who has been.

The reason that I say that is because someone who is abused physically or has been abused physically generally knows what to expect and they also know that they have and can survive it. For someone who lives with the threat of violence, without it actually happening; it becomes something of an unknown, which actually increases the level of fear.

What happens is that the victim then has to imagine what will happen if the abuse turns physical. When we imagine something that we fear we never imagine a best case scenario. We imagine the worst possible things that could happen, and then generally add a little more to that.

The fear of physical danger is a very powerful and controlling emotion. It has been used by people for centuries to achieve what they want from others simply because it is very powerful and effective.

In an abusive relationship this is a constant threat and obviously the victim is going to do all that they can to avoid it happening. This is the same whether there is violence or not.

Nobody wants to be beaten, and will do everything they need to, to avoid it happening. This is how an abuser uses the fear of physical abuse to control the victim.

Fear for the children

For this section we will assume that there are children in the relationship. When I am talking about fear for the children, I am not talking about the fear of danger to the children, which is generally a fear that will push someone to take action, what I am talking about is the fear of losing the children.

One of the things an abuser will tell the victim is that if they were to leave then they would lose the children. When you add to this that they are more than likely telling the victim what a terrible parent they are to begin with, and then add the threat of loosing the children, this becomes very real for the victim.

Then there is also the fact that they are not just losing the children, but that they will be leaving the children with the abuser, and nobody wants to do that to their children.

Now logic and reason tell us that if there is an abusive relationship and the victim does manage to break out, then there is not a lot of chance that the abuser will gain custody of the children, but they don't seem to realise this at the time because fear is a major factor and is clouding their minds.

We are going to talk about children in an abusive relationship a little later, but there is another point about children that is a factor in controlling the victim and that is generally people want their kids to grow up with two parents. It is not the main part of the fear, but it does play a part in the whole scheme of things so it is worth mentioning.

The primary part of this fear is losing the children if they were to leave the relationship. The abuser will tell the victim that if they leave they are not taking the kids. Obviously this becomes a big factor in keeping the victim in the relationship, and powerless to do much about it.

Fear for others

What I am talking about here is that if a victim was to escape from the relationship then they will need to go somewhere. Even if they were to go to a hostel there are still others that the abuser could get at in order to get at the victim.

Whether the other people are under physical threat or not, a victim will not want to take their problems to someone else's home. The abuser will be making it very clear that if the victim were to leave then they would chase them wherever they went.

You need to remember that once someone has control, the last thing that they want is to lose that control. They will do what they need to in order to keep that control. The other thing is that an abuser looks upon the victim as their property, and they do not want to lose anything that they own.

A victim will generally have family and friends that are known to the abuser, even with the isolation going on, and they do not want them to be involved in what will happen if the abuser does chase them. This is even more so if there is violence. The last thing anyone wants is to bring violence to someone else. Once again it only has to be the belief that this could happen that makes it real.

If you take away any kind of support network, which is what the isolation does, and then remove anyone else, that is left by making threats against them, then the victim is very quickly running out of options, as far as they can see.

Fear of retribution from others besides the abuser

If you take into account the things that we have talked about when it comes to isolation and also the fact that nobody knows what goes on behind closed doors, what you have is a situation where a victim is surrounded by people that do not believe that the abuser is the sort of person that would do that in the first place.

With the isolation that has been taking place it is common to find that most of the friends the victim has are essentially the abusers friends that have become the victim's friends.

I know I have mentioned it before and I will mention it again here as it is important to help point out how big a deal this can be.

Even though Ange's ex-husband was jailed for 5 years there are still so called friends of Ange that believe he was the victim and the whole thing was a plot by her to simply get him out of the house. They still do not believe he was capable of such a thing.

Now for us this is not really a big deal. Those people do not have anything to do with us and we do not have anything to do with them, however it can be very different and very difficult for some people in this situation.

The family and friends of the abuser will often side with them and can make things very uncomfortable for a victim. When you take into account the isolation that has happened through various means, it adds another level to the fears that a victim has, and something else that will keep them stuck in an abusive relationship.

Fear of failing in the relationship

This may sound a little strange to say in that the victim is not the one who failed in the relationship, it is the abuser. For the victim to breakout of the abuse, then they have to break the relationship. Strange as it may sound this is a very real fear.

Society tells us that when we enter into a long term relationship it is something that needs to be worked at and it is all too easy to walk away. The traditional wedding vows we are accustomed to states that we will stick by the partner and the relationship for better, for worse, for richer, for poorer etc. That is the basis of a long term relationship, whether the words have been said or not.

I have heard people use their wedding vows as an excuse to stay in an abusive relationship. They say something like – "when I took those vows, I meant them." I do not want to get into the argument about honouring vows and the high divorce rate and all that, but I do think that there is nowhere in the vows where it says anything about having to be treated like a slave and a victim by the partner and they have to stay in the relationship – no matter what. In fact the vows do talk about honouring each other and respecting each other. Surely an abuser is not taking their part of the vows all that seriously. You will often find that the abuser will quote these vows at the victim as another means of control; by telling them that they are breaking the vows that they made.

As I said it is not the vows that make the difference, it is the expectation that a long term relationship is based on the idea of the vows. As a society that has essentially been created by the church it has become part of the basic upbringing to think that a long term relationship is something that needs to be worked on, so therefore quitting on the relationship is the same as admitting that the victim has failed in keeping the relationship together.

It is never the abuser that leaves the victim; it is always the other way around. It is always the victim that has to be the one to finally leave the relationship and it is the victim that carries the failure of this relationship with them.

You have to remember that the abuser is drumming into the victim the whole time about how useless and worthless they are and that they are complete failures. To add another one to the list becomes a big deal. Perhaps it even goes as far as the victim being proud of the fact that despite everything they have managed to keep the relationship together.

Fear of being alone

When you take into account that the abuser will have been drumming into the victim how they are useless, ugly, fat and stupid and essentially stripping the victim of any kind of self-respect and dignity, then the fear of being alone for the rest of their lives becomes a very big deal.

It probably goes even further than that, the abuser has been in the victim's head for some time telling them that no one else would have them and how lucky they are to have the abuser in the first place. This is very much designed to make sure that the victim is afraid of spending the rest of their life alone.

By now the victim is feeling like the abuser wants them to and they do believe that they will spend the rest of their life alone, and it is scary enough to keep the victim in an abusive relationship.

Remember it does not have to be real in order for it to be a powerful controlling emotion in the victim's mind.

Fear of not being good enough without them

Another fear for a victim is that they are actually as useless and as stupid as the abuser repeatedly tells them they are.

During the relationship the abuser will not only assume control over the victim they will assume control over everything. What this means is that the victim is not really involved in any of the decision making and the running of the house and the family.

At the same time the abuser is telling the victim that they have to do everything themselves because the victim is not able to do it. What this does is makes the victim dependant on the abuser. I am not only talking about financial dependence, I am talking about being dependant on the abuser for simply surviving.

This covers everything from handling the money, paying the bills, general household repairs and all of the decision making that takes place.

Eventually the victim does come to see that they are dependent on the abuser for simply surviving and this then turns into the fear that they are not able to survive without the abuser being there to look after them.

Add this to the isolation, and it becomes a very big thing for the victim. They almost become a bit like a drone just doing what they are told by the abuser to do.

All the time the abuser is telling the victim how stupid and useless they are and how they are lucky to have the abuser there to take care of them.

In order for a victim to leave a relationship like this they need to realise they can take care of themselves and the kids if there are any, without the abuser. That is a big step for someone to make who has very little, if any, self-respect and dignity left to begin with.

Fear of looking like a fool

Pride is another part of a human being that plays a part in all of our lives. I am going to talk about this in more detail a little later, but for now I want to concentrate on the fact that it is a major fear for a victim when they are stuck in an abusive relationship.

In order to leave the relationship and start again the biggest thing they need to do is to admit that they failed. They have failed in the relationship, they have failed their partner, they have failed in their choice of partner, and they have failed to keep the family together. It is tough enough to admit this to themselves but to break out of the relationship, means that they have to admit it to everyone else.

Remember earlier we talked about excuses and how that in the beginning the victims believed them, but even after they stopped believing them, they still kept them up for the outside world, this point is essentially the follow on to that.

During an abusive relationship there will be those on the outside that are trying to talk to the victim and convince them that things are not working out and they should leave. During this time they will be using their excuses, defending their partner and pretending that it is not really that bad.

To actually leave the relationship is now the same as admitting to those on the outside that they were wrong and even if the on lookers do not say "I told you so" it is something that will be ringing inside the victim's mind.

This is essentially the part where pride can keep a victim in a relationship. There are others, but pride as well as the fear of ridicule and looking like a fool, is a very powerful driver.

If you are trying to help someone in an abusive relationship, this is something that you need to keep in mind. It is not an easy thing to try to help someone, who outwardly does not want help. There is a section later in the book about how you can help the victim; we will discuss how to overcome this fear then.

Fear of the unknown

One of the biggest fears that all people have is a fear of going into a situation that we do not know and even more so one where we are unable to predict the outcome.

In order for a victim to leave a relationship, that has been reasonably long term, there are so many things in the future that are complete unknowns; it can be scarier than the relationship they are in.

I think it is pretty clear how frightening this can be for anybody, but for someone who is constantly being mentally, emotionally and even physically abused, this is huge factor preventing them from going forward.

Summary

Throughout this chapter I have spoken a lot about the fears of a victim and about how powerful they can be in keeping them in an abusive relationship.

Fear is probably the most powerful emotion that people have and it can be both empowering and crippling. When the fears are based on the negative then they are perhaps as crippling for a person as losing the use of your legs. Fear has that much power over people.

On the other hand fear can also be a very strong driving force. It can be the fear of NOT doing something and the consequences that come from that which will push people to go well beyond their normal limits. A very quick example of this is for any parent, seeing their child in danger will spur them into action to protect the child at all costs. It is simply the fear of danger to the child that can create a powerful force within the parent. It could even be the same parents that are struck by the fears mentioned above, but will still react to a different kind of fear in the opposite way.

The thing with fear is that it can be used in a number of ways. The abuser uses the fear in the victim to keep them in the relationship and under control. It is as powerful as putting a chain around their leg and keeping them locked up.

You also need to keep in mind that the victim is not at their best emotionally and mentally to begin with, then when you add the fears that we have talked about on top of that it starts to make sense how someone can be absolutely trapped with nowhere to go.

When someone is lacking in self-respect and self-belief then all these things really do start to become like a solid wall.

It is when I think of these things as well as what the victim is going through that I start to think about how impressive the people who do manage to break out of these relationships really are. The thing is they are only people, and they did manage to find the courage despite everything to break free. If you are a victim and you are reading this please take some encouragement from this and do not think that those who have done it before you are any better than you, because they are not.

I am sure there are many other fears and doubts that go on within the victim, and I am only really able to cover some of the bigger ones in this book. I do hope that whilst reading through this you are starting to think a little deeper about all the things that are going on. I like to think that understanding and awareness is the first step to being able to do something about it. It is much easier to work with something when you understand it better.

Once again I do want to point out that not all people and situations are the same and the information in this book, whilst being accurate, is general. It is the ideas or principles that are important. You can take what is written here and apply the same kind of thinking to the specific situation you are dealing with.

Comfort Zones

This is a favourite topic of mine because I think that it is something that affects all of us throughout our lives. You may or may not have heard the expression before, but comfort zones are very much a part of human society in all forms.

A comfort zone is a conventional area of our lives where things are predictable and therefore there is no fear of the unknown. We are quite happy to live in this area because we can deal with what we know. It may be that we do not like the things that are part of the comfort zone, but we prefer those things to something that is outside of what we consider to be the norm.

Domestic abuse is related to this. This applies to the victim in that even though they are not happy being stuck in an abusive relationship, it is still preferred over having to break out of it and change it. You could say that it is like being stuck between a rock and a hard place; the other expression that would apply here is "better the devil you know".

What both of these things are saying is that although they are abused and mistreated, it is still a world that they know and understand and to a certain degree learn to control. They come to learn what the triggers are for the abuser and they try to avoid them.

In the previous chapter when I was talking about fear, there was one that I left out. It is one of the things that people fear almost as much as anything else and it is 'change'. It is not often talked about because it is not a single event as such. For example it is often said that people are afraid of dying and people are afraid of pubic speaking; but rarely is 'change' mentioned in that list.

Let me give you a simple example of what I am talking about here. People are essentially generally pretty predictable in what they will do in their everyday life. I am sure that when you look at the things in your day you will find that there are a lot of patterns that you repeat all the time, just because you are comfortable with that way of doing things. You will find that for your shopping you will go to the same store, and unless there is something dramatic that happens, you will still go to the same store, even though there is one around the corner that is cheaper or has a better range, and that is because you are comfortable in the store that you use.

How does it feel when you go into your usual store and find that they have moved things around? OK, it does not make you afraid but you don't like it. It is just not the same once that happens and the thing that kept you going there is no longer there and you may even change stores.

You see that with this small change, it upset something in you and you did not like it anymore, and that is because what you were used to and comfortable with had all of a sudden changed. This is a simple example of what change can mean, and I am sure that most people will relate to it on some level. What this is, is a comfort zone. You were comfortable in that environment and once it changed it was not the same and so you were forced out of your comfort zone and it would take a little time to get into a new one.

This same example applies right across our lives. It can be found in almost every aspect of our lives, in some degree or another. Let's have a look at a bigger example and see how it can become really intrusive.

One of the more prominent examples of where a comfort zone will stop people from making a change is with their job. How many people do you know who are in a job that they hate. I am sure they could find another job, but as soon as you suggest that to them they start coming out with a hole range of excuses as to why they need to stay where they are. It could be anything from the travel distance, the hours, the money and a thousand others. But what it really comes down to, if you think about it, is the fact that even though they are not happy where they are, they would rather stay there, in the comfort zone, than move outside of it and get a new job.

Being stuck in a domestic abuse relationship is no different in that it is the place where the victim understands the world and even though they do not like it, it is still a comfort zone for them, and it is easier than having to face a different future outside of that comfort zone.

They may wish it was different, and they may like to think that there are many things that are keeping them there, but when it really comes down to it, it is the concept of comfort zones and fear of change that is the main thing that is keeping them there.

I am sure they can create all sorts of barriers and reasons to stay, and some of them may well be valid, I am not saying that there are not valid reasons in some cases, but if you really start to push them to provide the reasons, I am sure that you can break them all down a little at a time and demonstrate that they are not really barriers, but excuses to avoid change.

I am not suggesting that they are staying because they want to; I am saying that the fear of change and the thought of pushing out of a comfort zone is very much a part of who we are and it is perhaps the biggest barrier that you will come across.

Once again it is being made aware of this that is the key to solving it. Even then it is still part of your life, it does not go away and we need to be constantly reminded that it is almost a natural tendency to get caught in this trap, and unless we are prepared to push out of the comfort zone then we will remain trapped. It does not matter what we are talking about here, it could be simply shopping in the same store, a job, a relationship – regardless of whether it is abusive or not.

It does go against basic human nature to break free of a comfort zone and face change, but it is something we must all do in order to move forward with our lives.

WHAT'S LEFT WHEN YOUR SELF-RESPECT IS TAKEN?

This is a really important question when you think about it. One of the things that define us as people is the respect that we have for ourselves and those around us. That is what basically makes a community work – respect. I am going to try and confine this to self-respect and look at how a victim in an abusive relationship essentially has this stripped away from them.

When you get down to the level that is just above self-preservation the thing that makes us fight for ourselves is our self-respect and our sense of dignity and worth. What I mean by that is that it is when we feel we have been slighted at an emotional level that we feel the need to fight back. In order to feel that we have been slighted at an emotional level we need to have a degree of self-respect.

Basically in this context it is self-respect that will cause a person to think something like, I deserve better than that, I need to be treated better and that kind of thought. The problem is that an abuser will slowly strip away this sense of self-respect and dignity to get to the point where the victim no longer believes that they do deserve to be treated any better than they are being treated.

When I am talking about self-respect I do not want it to be confused with the ego. Although it is true to say that the ego is a sense of our self-worth as a person, I am talking about something that is a little deeper than that. You could say that it is our self-respect that we use as a measuring stick in terms of how we allow ourselves to be treated. I know there is a lot more to all of this than I am talking about here, but for the purposes of this book, I am trying to keep it in terms of how the victim allows these things to happen to them without fighting back, and that is simply because their self-respect has been eroded by the abuser and by the abusive relationship.

We have already spoken about how this happens in terms of the abuser trying to make sure they are in control of the victim. This is done by inflating their own position whilst at the same time reducing the victim's position, therefore the effect is doubled.

The thing is that when the self-respect and sense of self dignity are gone the fight is gone. That is ultimately what the abuser is looking for; because once this happens they have almost complete domination. They don't even need to fight for it anymore.

The big problem that you have when a victim reaches this point is that they have almost given up trying to find a way out and have become resigned to the fact that they are not worthy of anymore than they have in the relationship. It is not only the fight against the abuser that is gone; it is the fight for something better that is gone also.

However that does not mean that it cannot be brought back; it is just going to take a lot of work and effort on the part of the victim and some help from someone who is patient and understanding to help them get it back.

Chances are that at this point there is also a degree of depression involved. When a victim reaches this point they no longer believe that they deserve more than what the relationship is giving them; and therefore they do not feel worthy of anymore either.

What happens now is that the victim essentially goes into survival mode and focuses their energy on getting through what has become their life, abuse included.

You can see how the pattern sort of works. Throughout all the different stages in the relationship there are different things that keep them there, but ultimately they get worn down by the abuser to the point where they do not fight anymore, because they do not believe they even have a right to fight anymore.

This all sounds very bleak for the victim, and it most certainly is, but it does not mean that it is the end. There is a road back from this point, and things can change. Like I said earlier, as long as they still draw breath, it can change. There is always a spark inside that with the right fanning can ignite again and there is a way out from there. If you are a victim and you are reading this, I hope this will encourage you to start looking for that spark within yourself, which is the first step in breaking free – finding the spark and finding the person that you once were. From there you can grow again.

FAILURE IS A BIG PART OF THE PICTURE

I touched on this subject a bit earlier when I was talking about the fear of failure and the fear of looking like a fool, but I think that is a core part of what is going on inside the victim that we need to take more time to look into this further.

When talking about fears, there was one that I did not talk about much and that is the fear of failure. Along with the fear of change, the fear of failure will bring someone to a complete stop in their life, because failure is seen as a very negative thing in society.

When you start to think about it failure is shunned at every level of society and it is something that all people avoid at all costs. The problem being that it has become such a big deal that it is now considered better not to try than it is to try and fail.

You may be thinking that this is not exactly true, but when it comes down to it, it really is. Let me give some examples of what I am talking about here.

The school grades came out a couple of weeks ago. In the paper were the usual articles about the top scorers, the best schools and all that kind of thing. It is strange that there was not a single article about the students, who against the odds worked their guts out in order to get passable grades in order to pursue their ambitions and get on the university courses that they wanted. The reason for this is because society celebrates success. I agree that those who got the grades they needed were successful, but they were not the best.

I once heard a sportsman talking about the medals in the Olympics. He said that to win a bronze metal was better than winning a silver medal because when you win silver, you lose to whoever came first, but when you win bronze, you beat everyone else. In a way it sort of makes sense, but it also shows how it is success that is celebrated, in all things.

In Australia they stopped the kid's sports being scored for

under 12's. The reason for this was because those that did not win would get upset about it, and it is better not to score than it is to have losers. Once again showing it is success that matters, and failure should be swept under the carpet and disregarded.

Let's look at the Wright brothers. Everyone knows they were the first ones to build an aeroplane that could fly. What about all of the people that had tried to do it before they finally hit on the right solution? How many of the ideas. from those early attempts finally led the Wright brothers to their design? I am sure you could find out somewhere, but the point is it is not well known because although they tried, and got better each time, they weren't the ones that were successful therefore nobody knows their name.

I think I have made the point here that in our world it is success that is rewarded and celebrated and it is failure that is shunned and ignored. So now we can get back to the main point of this chapter.

In a relationship there are many expectations placed on the people involved to succeed in not only the relationship as a whole, but also in fulfilling their role in the partnership, and if there are kids, as a parent. All of these things are measured on a success and failure scale. No matter what other circumstances are involved you are either a success or failure.

Keeping in mind that we are talking from the victim's point of view here; then it is the responsibility of the victim to make sure that their partner is happy in the relationship and is getting all the things out of it that they need. When the abuser is blaming them for all of the bad things in the relationship they are telling them that they are failing in their duty to make sure that the abuser is happy. That is why they are angry and nasty all of the time, because the victim is a failure as a partner.

If there are children involved then it is the victim's responsibility to be a good parent and make sure that the family stays together. If the victim is not able to keep the family together then they are failing as a partner and as a parent and they are robbing the children of one of their parents.

Then there is the relationship itself. If the victim were to leave the relationship, then they are failing in that as well.

Given that society is based on celebrating success and frowning upon failure all of these things are very strong motivators to keep a victim in a relationship in order to make it not fail. I know it may look a little trivial when it is written here in simple terms like this, but I do not want you to underestimate the power that this has over a person.

I do not know of a single person that would condemn a victim for getting out of an abusive relationship and I am sure that society would encourage and help anyone who is in an abusive relationship to break free of it, but nonetheless the whole success and failure thing is a huge weight that is carried by the victim.

The abuser is telling them they are failing as a partner and if there are kids the abuser will most certainly be pointing out that they are also failing as a parent, therefore the thought of failing even more by not keeping the family together really adds a huge pressure to the victim.

Please do not dismiss this as it is a very big piece of the puzzle that should be taken into account. If you are a victim reading this, I want you to know that it is not you who is failing in all these areas; it is the abuser that is failing. They are not living up to their part of the relationship. What about their part of making sure that you are happy and getting all that you need? What about their part in being a parent and teaching the children how they should be respectful of other people. If the relationship fails, it fails because they are unable to live in a loving and respectful relationship. It is the abuser that is the failure, not the victim. Please think about that.

PRIDE – ENEMY AND SAVIOUR

I have been looking forward to writing this chapter as I think that pride is one of the keys things in a person. I believe that a person's sense of pride is one of the things that is a very major part in their life. As with all things it can be a very positive force and it can also be a very negative force.

The best place to begin this chapter is to define exactly what pride is and how it is such an integral part of the things that makes us the people that we are.

To me pride is that thing inside you that you measure yourself against. I guess you could call it a sort of baseline or yard stick by which you try to live your life. To me it is a little different from self-respect in that pride is the baseline that your self-respect helps you to maintain. In other words when you allow yourself to be treated below your level of self-respect, it is your level of pride that you measure it against and basically come away feeling disappointed with yourself.

The same works the other way, when you do something that is above the level that your pride is set at then you feel proud of yourself for achieving that.

For example when I do something I always try and do it to the best of my ability. It does not matter what it is, if I want to do it in the first place or if I am any good at it. The thing I always aim for is to do my best. When I finish something, as long as I am satisfied that I have done all that I could, then I feel proud of the thing that I have done. On the other hand on those rare occasions when I do something with a mediocre amount of effort, but still get the desired result, I do not get a lot from it, because I know that I did not give it all I had.

When you look at that example what you have is someone who is very driven to achieve and does the best that they can do. I have very high expectations of myself and I push myself to achieve them. This is generally a good thing, but it can also be a negative thing. For example I did say that it did not matter what

I was doing, this makes me very competitive, and perhaps a little too much at times.

So you can see there are good points and bad points to this, and this is the same when it comes to a victim in an abusive relationship. The title of this chapter states that pride is the enemy and the saviour, and this is how it works.

Firstly let's look at how pride can be the enemy. The first thing to look at is the previous chapter about failure. Everyone of us has a sense of pride therefore when it comes to the victim it can become a point of pride that no matter how bad things were at home and how badly they were treated, they were still able to keep things together, they were still able to be a partner and parent. The down side of this is that they are using it in order to continue the relationship and therefore continue the abuse. It is the pride in the fact of not failing that stops them from leaving the relationship and taking action against the abuser.

On the other hand it is that same pride that keeps them going. Despite all the things that are going on and no matter how bad things were and how much abuse they had to deal with, they are able to keep going, and they pride themselves on that. It could also be that no matter how bad the abuser was, the victim was still able to keep going – in spite of them.

Those two paragraphs essentially say the same things but with a different twist and a different angle on how the pride is being used. That is how pride is both a saviour and an enemy. It is the saviour part that I do want to focus on though.

I talked earlier about how the self-respect gets taken away and leaves the victim almost nowhere, well the thing with pride is that although it may diminish, it never goes completely and therefore it can be awakened and used as a tool and a weapon for the victim to fight their way out of an abusive relationship.

The victim should take pride in the fact that against all the odds, and no matter how bad things got, they stuck it out and they carried on. You could almost say that is a win over the abuser.

But you should not allow your pride to keep you there. You should use your pride to re-grow your self-respect and your dignity and use this strength to make the changes necessary to get out of the relationship.

Don't let pride stand in your way of getting out. Use your pride in yourself to do something about it. Trust me when I tell you, you will feel much prouder of yourself when you can look back and think that regardless of what the abuser did and how much they manipulated you, you were still able to stand up to them. You were able to overcome all the things they did, you were able to conquer the fears they created in you and you were strong enough to break free.

It is that kind of pride that you want to be feeling. You do not want to hang on to the pride of hanging in there; that is called being a martyr; using your pride to justify being a victim. That is what martyrdom is all about; being proud of allowing yourself to become a victim and not giving in; in spite of the suffering that you had to endure. That is a negative use of pride, because there is no gain from it, for anyone.

In the case of a victim in an abusive relationship that kind of pride is not something that you want to be feeling. If this is one of the reasons that you are staying then you should sit back and have a think about who is gaining from you doing this?

If you are not a victim and you are trying to help someone in an abusive relationship, then the ideas in this chapter are a great thing to talk to the victim about. The thing with pride is that it can be awakened and it can be used as a base for the rebuilding a person's self-respect and dignity and from there also follows the strength to do something about it.

What about the Kids

Throughout this book I have tried to be mindful of various of relationships. I do not want this book to become focused on a purely male/female relationship, but I do think it is important that when looking at abusive relationships I include some information for when children are involved. I am putting this in the victim section because I do believe that even if they are not directly abused, they are still victims when they are caught in an abusive relationship.

As much as a victim will protest that the kids are not victims and that if they were to become victims then they would do something about it, I am going to tell you that anyone who is surrounded by anger, negativity and abuse, whether it is directed at them or not is a victim in the overall scheme of things.

Children encounter many challenges while growing up even at the best of times, when you add a domestic abuse situation to this I think that just adds a whole new dimension to things. When there is an abusive relationship and children there are a lot of things that change, including the way that the parent behaves towards the children, the things they will let them get away with.

That is not to mention the things that the children are learning from the behaviour that is around them. I am going to talk about a few specific things here; as I am sure there are many that do not realise the impact that an abusive relationship can have on children. If they do realise it, perhaps they do not actually think about the bigger picture.

Parenting in an Abusive Situation

What I want to talk about in this section is how parents in an abusive relationship tend to be different parents than they would be in a different situation.

The biggest difference in an abusive relationship is that the parents tend to parent in such a way as to keep the children out of the way of the abuser and do more to placate the children and keep the peace than they necessarily would in a different situation.

A victim in an abusive relationship works on the premise that if the abuser is not angry and upset, and therefore getting things their own way, then it is less likely that they will get more abuse for the time being. What this means is that in order to make sure that the abuser is not upset, by anything, the victim will often do all they can in order to make the children happy, and if possible less conspicuous in the overall scheme of things.

There is another reason for this, apart from self-preservation, in that if the children do not make the abuser angry then they are less likely to be on the receiving end of abuse.

The other thing that the victim will do for the children is to be less strict with the children. There are a couple of reasons for this, firstly they have enough problems with the abuser being angry and upset with them, so they do not want to bring anymore of that on themselves, and the other is because in a sense they are apologising to the children and compensating for the way that the home life is.

You have to remember that the victim believes that they are the cause of the majority of the problems in the relationship, and therefore they not only behave in such a way as to keep the peace, they act in a way to almost compensate the children for what they are missing out on; namely a loving and happy home.

The other thing that you have to remember is that the victim is not encouraged or even accustomed to being a dominant personality, and therefore they tend to be passive, all of which the child comes to learn and take advantage of, as all kids will do.

So what this essentially means is that the children do not receive the discipline that they need. The victim protects them from the abuser and at the same time fails to provide the discipline themselves.

I am not trying to say that any of this is intentional on the part of the victim, but what I am trying to say that if you look closely you will see that all of this is a natural extension of the things that we have been talking about throughout this book.

Another thing with children that are surrounded by domestic abuse is that their parents are essentially the role models that they build their foundations on. You may remember that we spoke earlier how people come into a relationship with a history and ideas on how a relationship should be etc. well the foundation for that comes from childhood.

What they are being taught

Children learn from not only what they are taught, they learn a lot more form their environment and the things that are going on around them. The things that happen in the early years of their lives are things that they are going to take with them for the rest of their lives. It is during childhood that our idea of 'normal' gets implanted. The environment that your children spend their early years in is the one that stays with them.

Is the relationship and the environment in which the children are being raised the one that you want them to build their concept of relationships?

I do not think that I need to wait for an answer on that question. The point however is; this is exactly where this information comes from for the children. I am sure that they are encouraged to think differently by the parents, but do as I say and not as I do has always been a poor substitute for modelling the correct behaviour, and always will be.

If we look at an abusive relationship and the children that are involved you will notice that the children tend to follow the gender example that is being set for them by the parents. In that if the mother is the victim, the daughter(s) will learn from this that either that is the way they should expect to be treated by their partner in the future, or they will go the other way and become much more dominant towards their partner in the future, and can even go to the opposite extreme and become abusers.

The same thing applies to the male children; they will either follow the father's example or swing completely the opposite way. However if the male is the abuser, it is more likely that the son(s) will follow this example. It may even happen before they grow to have adult relationships.

You can see that not only are the children being treated differently by their parents, they are also learning from the example that is set by them.

Even if the children are not directly abused, it does not mean that they are not still victims. Just as you do not need bruises to be abused, you also do not need to be directly abused to be effected by what is going on, which essentially becomes abuse in the form of not creating a good environment for the children to grow up in.

Does the victim have more than one abuser?

I am including this section just to give you something else to think about in terms of what the children are learning. As the children grow in an abusive environment they will follow the lead of one of the parents or the other, as mentioned earlier. This is not just confined to future relationships; this is also with respect to the victim and abuser in the form of the parents.

We have discussed in detail how a victim basically becomes lacking in self-respect and dignity and adopts a very passive role in the relationship; which the children pick up on.

As the children grow and become teenagers, they come to

realise that the victim, who in this case is a parent, is a person that can be bullied and controlled. What this means is that the children can also take advantage of this situation.

Not only does this mean that the victim is abused by the partner and now the children, it also reinforces the situation in the child's mind and becomes something that they will almost certainly be taking into future relationships with them.

It is clear that it is not just the parent that becomes the victim of the young abuser; chances are if there are siblings of the same gender as the victim, they will also be on the receiving end of the abuse.

Two Parents don't always mean it is better

As you can see from the things that I have spoken about in this chapter, the effect of growing up in the environment of an abusive relationship, whether they are direct victims or not, is something that has much further reaching effects than appears on the surface.

Earlier we spoke about the fact that the victim will often stay in an abusive relationship in order to keep the family together and therefore protect the children from growing up with only one parent, but I have to say that you are doing the children a huge disservice by doing this.

Leaving an abusive relationship will teach your children a much better lesson than staying in this environment. Firstly you are teaching them that it is not OK to treat other people in this manner. By not staying and not tolerating it, you are not validating it in their minds.

Secondly by getting the courage to do something about the way things are, you are telling them that it is not OK to be a victim. Once again, by taking a stand and making the hard decision, you are letting you children know that they do not have to allow anyone to treat them in that manner.

Staying in an abusive relationship is not doing the children any favours in any way. In fact it doing far more damage that you know.

As a parent, I am sure that you want your children to have the best opportunities in life as you can; do that by demonstrating some very major things that they will take forward with them. The message they take forward with them is the one that is demonstrated to them each and every day as they are growing up.

Just because there are two parents does not mean that home life or the children's up bringing is better. In fact sometimes it is a lot worse.

If you are a victim that is reading this, an abuser or someone who is on the outside, there is one major question that everyone should be asking themselves and that is - What example or message do you want to convey to your children?

BARRIERS

In this chapter I want to talk about how people create barriers in order to protect themselves. You may think that this seems a natural thing to do, but the point of this chapter is that more often than not people need to protect themselves from themselves more than they do from the outside world.

The problem with barriers is that what they effectively do is remove options. When we remove our options for ourselves, it means we cannot make choices. What this ultimately leads to is that if we do not have any choice then we do not have to take responsibility for the way things are.

The difference with barriers and excuses is that barriers generally come in the form of something tangible and the main difference is that the person who creates the barriers believes them. Excuses on the other hand are not always believed by the person making the excuses, although sometimes they are.

When I talk about barriers I am talking about the things that we all like to put in place so that we do not have to do something we should do. It could be anything from changing jobs, leaving a relationship, or many other things.

Barriers do not do have to be created by the person that is trapped by them, they can be put there by someone or something else. But they still do the same thing. They stop someone from doing something, because as far as they are aware it is not possible to do it, because of the barriers.

There is something else that has a lot in common with barriers and that is fear. I like to think of barriers as being the manifestation of something that enables us to give into our fears without having to confront the fear in the first place.

I know this is all getting a little philosophical, but I will give you some examples that will help to explain what I am talking about.

I have used one example already in this book when I was

talking about how someone will put barriers in the way so as to retain their comfort zone and not have to change jobs. Let me refresh your memory on that a little.

I am sure that you all know someone who is always complaining and moaning about their job. However when you suggest to them that they change jobs they are very reluctant to do so. The first things that you get are the excuses, and then once the excuses are out of the way then you get the barriers.

The excuses tend to be reasons why they cannot change or do not want to change jobs in the first place. Things like I will look for another job soon, I just want to stay for the time being because I have that holiday booked. I am going to wait and see what happens when the pay reviews come round. I am in line for that promotion. These are all excuses for them to stay in the current job, even if they do hate it.

If you can get past the excuses, and they do start looking for another job, then you get to the barriers. The barriers are then the reasons why they can't take the new job. Too far to travel, not enough benefits, not the direction I want to take, the hours are too hard to work with. These are the reasons, or excuses to stop them from moving forward, in other words they are barriers that stop someone from taking the step, even if it presented to them.

You see the excuses are used in order to justify not trying; the barriers are used to stop moving forward, once the excuses have been removed. In this example the barriers are used to rule out the new job as being a viable option. So what that does is allows the person to justify to themselves why they are still "stuck" in the job they are in.

If you take this understanding of excuses and barriers and apply them to the victim of domestic abuse we will see how it enables them to justify staying in the relationship, without having to confront the fact that they do have choices.

Before I carry on with this, I want to point out that these things are not conscious decisions on the part of people. We do not know that we are creating the barriers for ourselves; we honestly believe that these things do prevent us from moving forward. I am not suggesting for a moment that a victim is staying in a relationship because they want to; I am suggesting that they believe they do not have any options. Without options, there is not a choice to be made.

The other thing that I should point out here is that sometimes the barriers are in fact valid and real. Just because someone is using a list of barriers does not mean that they are not real. I guess the real test comes when the barrier is put under scrutiny and testing then it becomes quite obvious whether it is a real barrier, or simply an excuse in disguise.

The barriers are put in place by the victim, we have read all of what has been said about the fears and state of mind of the victim, and so it is only natural that these are going to manifest as very real barriers for the victim. You also need to remember that the abuser will also be helping the victim in maintaining the barriers that are keeping them there.

One of the barriers that I encounter more often than not is the fact that the victim simply cannot afford to leave, financially. On the surface this is very real, and it is only when you really start looking at it, that you come to see that there are ways around it.

Money is a very big factor is all our lives, and as much as someone will tell you that money does not make the world go round, it is not really that true anymore. I am as romantic as the next person, but the reality is that no matter what, we need money to survive that is the truth of the matter.

The thing with the money barrier is that there are ways to overcome it. We live in a world where there is generally welfare available to everyone. It can be hard work to get at it, and there are a number of hoops that you may need to jump through, but ultimately it is there and can be used to support someone. Even if it is only a transition phase, it is available. I m not suggesting this is the only answer and it is not a very valid barrier. I put it here to simply bring it to your attention, and therefore something to think about.

Another barrier that I encounter is the "I have nowhere to go". Once again, there are options out there for someone who is really serious about making a move. Not all of them are pretty, and not all of them are ideal, but once again for a short term and to help in the transition, there are still options.

Not being able to move out of the area because of family, friends, work, schools etc. Once again you have to think in terms of what is important. Staying in an abusive relationship, or struggling through a time of transition in order to reclaim your life.

There are many barriers that people will use for all sorts of things. Some of them are valid, but most of them are not. My best suggestion if you are faced with someone who is making the barriers is to talk them through the barrier and try and help them see that it is not as bad as it seems. A barrier that is not real will not stand up to close scrutiny and will crumble very quickly when you start to apply some logic and reason. The best way that you can break down the barriers, is to hit them with a good dose of reality. No believed barrier will stand up to a good pounding by reality.

There is something that you also need to be aware of if you are trying to help someone break down their barriers, and that is that generally they will not want them broken down. This requires a little time and patience to do. It is something that you need to be subtle about. A sledge hammer approach will not work here.

You almost have to guide someone to seeing the barrier for what it is and the best way to do that is to simply suggest ways around it and leave them to reach the ultimate conclusion.

You will notice that I have not spoken about how to break down our own barriers here, and that is because it is very, very hard to do, and most people simply cannot or will not do it themselves. You have to remember the barriers were created in the first place by us in order to justify something that we want. If you think about it, it takes something to trigger a change in thinking for us to be able to do it for ourselves, which is what I have suggested here.

The aim of this chapter is once again to provide information. I am sure that after reading it you will see where other people use barriers all the time, and you may even see some that you have used yourself, but this is going to be one of those things that OTHER people are guilty of using.

I am not different from anyone else in that respect. I know that I have used barriers in the past to justify things, and I know that I am more than likely doing it even now, in fact I know that I have a couple of barriers that I put in place for myself right now. And if I am honest I am going to do it some more in the future. It is human nature to be able to justify things to ourselves. It is tough to look at ourselves and be completely honest, I know there are people who think they are honest with themselves, but it is very few who can really take this on. All I am suggesting here is that it is part of what we do as people, and it is not something that is going to stop. If you can see the barriers that you create for yourself and can do something about it, then that is great, even if it is only for some things.

The best way to deal barriers is to understand them, or at the very least understand that they are there, and try to help others with their barriers. You will be amazed how much helping someone else with their issues will make you realise your own issues and barriers. Sometimes it is quite scary, and sometimes it shakes our own view of ourselves a little, but anything that makes us stop and think about ourselves and our lives in total honesty is nothing but a good thing. In fact, I think it is about the best thing that anyone can do for themselves.

SURVIVAL MODE

What eventually happens to the victim in a domestic abuse situation is that the victim goes into what is called a survival mode. What this means is that effectively the victim does not think about anything other than getting through each day the best that they can.

This is what happens once the hope finally disappears, they are stripped of their self-respect and dignity and basically become a shell of a person that only really thinks about one thing, and that is surviving each day.

I know that the picture I am painting is pretty grim and sounds a bit extreme but in essence that is what happens. The victim stops thinking about the future, stops thinking about things getting better, stops thinking about changing the situation, stops thinking about fighting back and most importantly stops thinking about breaking free.

They come to accept that this is their lot in life, and quite frankly they do not deserve any better than this anyway. It could get to the point where they think suicide is their only way out. When someone gets to this stage it is very hard to convince them that their life is worth living and that a better life is possible and accessible to them.

Their world comes to the point where they get through each day trying as much as possible to avoid the wrath of the abuser so that life can be bearable.

At this stage the abuser has effectively created a slave; someone who is there at their every whim. Regardless of what it is or what else is going on, their slave is there to do what they are told, they do not argue and fight back. The other thing is that there is no-one to question what the abuser is doing. It could be having an affair, it could be not working, it could be spending all of the income on drugs and drink, it does not really matter, because the victim has learned that that there is simply nothing they can do about it.

The problem with this is that there is now nothing that is going to change for the victim, except perhaps an escalating the abuse. There is one thing that is not constant throughout the whole relationship and that is the amount of abuse. Generally speaking the level of abuse is always increasing and this does not change just because the victim does not resist the abuser anymore. It has now become a way of life for the victim and the abuser, and it is not likely to change. It is very rare that the abuser will suddenly realise what has been happening, if the victim has come to accept this lifestyle, then it is going to take something extraordinary for anything to change.

Extraordinary things can and do happen so this does not mean that it is the end of the world. I will talk a little more about this a little later, but I wanted to use this chapter to make sure that everyone understands where all of the things that we have been talking about eventually lead to.

Earlier on I spoke about life being a conveyer belt and taking us all somewhere, all the time. Well when in a situation where there is domestic abuse this is where the conveyer belt will be leading the victim to. Ideally they will do something about it before it gets to this point, and step off the conveyer, but it does not happen very often.

Survival mode is helpful in that it does allow people to simply survive what they have to, the thing about it is that people get used to this being the way of life, and therefore the comfort zone, so it is very hard to snap out of it. However even though it is very hard, it is not impossible. Keep that in mind, nothing is impossible whilst we are alive and things can always change for the better.

IT NO LONGER EVEN OCCURS TO THEM TO LEAVE

I have put this in a separate chapter as it is a very important point that I want to make. When you look at the chapter on barriers and the chapter on survival mode you will see that at some point leaving simply is not an option.

A person can get so downtrodden and so degraded that they simply come to believe that they really are no good as a person and that they are in fact lucky to have what little they have in this life. Once someone is thinking like this, then not only do they not think of changing it, it's simply no longer an option that they even consider.

It goes far beyond making excuses, giving in to the fears, living in hope and denial, creating barriers, and all of the other things that we have spoken of. It simply does not even enter the head of the victim that they can or even should do anything to change the situation, let alone leave the abuser.

This is important to understand because when you are on the outside looking in, the first thing that occurs to you when you think of domestic abuse is 'why don't they just leave?' I hope by the time you reach this chapter you no longer think of it in terms of that simplified solution, but most importantly you come to understand that at some point it is not even a realistic option as far as the victim is concerned.

Trying to talk someone into leaving by the time they get to this point is extremely difficult to do. It is something that needs to be done very carefully and with sensitivity. There are so many others things that need to happen before this even becomes an option again, in that there is a lot of work to do with the victim in terms of rebuilding them as a person before this option can even be considered again.

I am going to talk a lot more about how you can help a victim in a domestic abuse situation, but I think that you need to bear in mind that once a victim has reached survival mode, simply leaving is really no longer an option as far as they are concerned and there is work that needs to be done before this option is available to them again.

But it can be done, always keep in mind that these things can be done, and there is always hope. Never give up completely, whether you are the victim or you are trying to help a victim, there is always hope.

Keep in mind that just as your self-respect and dignity was taken from you, it can also be retrieved. These things come from within, they are part of the self, and as long as there is a self, then these things can be cared for, nourished and re-grown.

SOME PEOPLE ARE ALWAYS VICTIMS

I am putting this chapter in here because I really want people to think about this. It is not necessarily directly related to domestic abuse but I think that it is important that people take a few minutes to think about themselves and their lives.

Once again I will point out that I am not here to make any judgements, my only goal throughout this book is to provide information that will help people and encourage them to think a little deeper about these things and perhaps form their own view based on the information discussed.

Have you ever noticed that there are some people that are always victims in one way or another? I am not just talking about those people who think they are victims because they do not want to accept responsibility for themselves and their own lives; I am talking about those people who just seem to attract trouble in one form or another.

It seems to me that there are those people who for one reason or another, no matter what they do; always seem to be on the receiving end of negative things. I have a theory about this. I think that this has a lot to do with personalities of people and also the attitude that they portray. This may sound a little weird but what I am talking about here is that people often get treated in a certain way because of the kind of people that they are or the vibes they give out.

Let me try and give you an example that will explain this. I am sure we all know someone who is generally very gentle and quite passive, a good and kind person who will do whatever they can to help anyone.

I am also sure that you have noticed that these people will be taken advantage of by people a lot of the time. I do know people like this, and I know that it happens.

On the other hand there are people we know who are the not so passive type, can be quite opinionated, still good people, but not the kind that is going to get taken advantage of easily.

Have you ever noticed then that it is generally the person in the first instance that always has the bad stuff happen to them?

The next part of this theory is that as people we are giving out all kinds of signals all the time that are picked up on by the people around us, whether we know them or not. We are doing the same to other people, whether we know them or not, we just get sort of a vibe from them and then we generally treat them according to the vibe that we have picked up on. None of this is happening consciously, it just sort of happens without anyone really noticing.

There is a little experiment and I guess you could call it a game that I like to play using this very thing. What I like to do is when I am in a crowded place like a train station or shopping centre I like to watch people moving through the crowd. You can see the sort of vibes that people are giving out simply by the way that the other people move around them.

I like to test this theory by picking a busy spot, squaring up my shoulders, looking determinedly straight ahead and walking in a straight line. I am not being aggressive or pushy, simply walking. It is quite amazing to see that almost all of the people will move out of my way. On the other hand if I start by looking down, and doing the side stepping, then I find that it is me that is doing all of the moving out of the way.

It is an interesting experiment, although not very scientific, but it does show that the signals we give out do make a difference to how the world treats us.

The point that I am trying to make is that you should be aware of the message that you are giving out and make sure they are in line with the way that you want to be treated by other people. It does not mean you have to be aggressive and thuggish in your approach to other people, but if you are confident and self assured, it will make a very big difference.

On the other hand if you are shy and timid, then people will know that they can take advantage of you and will treat you accordingly. It happens all the time.

I am not suggesting that people want to be victims, and I am not saying that people ask for what they get, I am simply saying that this is the way that the world works, and the first step is to understand that it is happening and then you can think about what signal you are giving out.

If you are a victim, and this goes for those that are victims in domestic abuse, you need to start thinking about the messages that you are giving out, not just at home but at all times with all interactions and I am sure that if you work at this you will notice a very big difference in your world.

I am not suggesting that it is going to solve your problem, but it certainly will help. This is something to think about and something to be aware of.

SOMETHING FOR THE VICTIM TO THINK ABOUT

In this chapter I am going to be talking directly to the victims. If you are not a victim, but are trying to help someone who is a victim then I hope that you will also get something from this; even if it gives you some ideas and pointers on some of the things that you can say. There is a section later in this book that is aimed at helping those who are helping victims, but there is still good information to be had from here also.

By the time that you reach this chapter there will be one of three things that have happened as you have been reading this book. Either you think it is absolute rubbish, and therefore will probably not reach this chapter or you will be reading it thinking that some of it sounds like it could be true, and you can see how these things can happen, even though things are certainly not like that for you.

You will have been thinking about the things that I have been talking about and relating to some if not all of it. If this is the case then most of the things will have come almost as a surprise for you.

One of the first things that someone will do in that last situation is to start blaming themselves for not seeing what had been happening. There are a couple of things that I want to point out before you start beating yourself up over this.

It is not normal for most people to think about things at this level. The second thing to be aware of is that as most people do not stop to think about things in this level of detail, for someone to do it for their own lives is very rare indeed. The point that I am trying to make here is that there is no reason that you would think about all of the things that I have been writing here in the first place, so there is no reason to be blaming yourself for not seeing it.

If you are now thinking about all of the things that I have been talking about and you are now seeing how many of the things relate to you, the next obvious question has to be – what can you do about it?

Now that you have reached the first point and realised firstly that your relationship is an abusive one and also that some of the other things have also been happening to you; I offer you my congratulations. This is not unlike and alcoholic admitting they have a problem with drink. It is the first step on the road to recovery, but it is only the first step, there is a lot more work to do yet.

I think that one of the best things that you can do is to get some help, even if it is only moral support and someone you can talk to about the problem, find someone who will help you. It does not have to be a professional, or even one of the many organisations that are out there, it could be a friend or family member. One thing that you do need to look out for is someone who is going to be able to understand your situation and help you to move forward, not someone who is going to help you wallow in your misery. That is not the way to move forward, it will only move you backward.

Throughout this book I have spoken about the rebuilding process. I am not talking about rebuilding your life after you make the changes to your current situation, what I am talking about is the restoration and nurturing of yourself that needs to take place within yourself in order to get the strength and courage to do what you need to do to move away from this relationship.

I think that you do need to think in terms of moving away from the relationship rather than thinking about repairing it. I am not going to say that these things cannot be fixed, but you need to be honest with yourself and realise that in reality you have tried to repair things in the past without success.

All the things that we have spoken about with regards to fear, excuses, and barriers are all things that do still need to be overcome in order for you to be able to break fee. The way that things are overcome is by you rebuilding your strength and confidence so you can push through all of those things. It has to come from within you, there is no one else that can make the changes and break free for you.

The next step is realising and admitting that you do have a problem and start thinking that you do deserve better than you have. This is a very important part of the whole process. You have to believe that you as a person deserve to be treated better than you are being treated and that you are going to make sure that you are. This is very easy for me to write in a few sentences but it is very different for someone who is reading this, it is a very big step.

Here is something that you should think about when you are thinking about all this, what if you had a close friend or relative that was being treated the way that you are being treated. Would you be happy about it?

What would you say to that person if they told you that you should not worry about them, they are only getting treated the way that they deserve, and it is not something that you should worry about? It is amazing how much it changes when it is someone else that we are talking about isn't it.

Here is a little trick that people should be using all the time in their lives and that is to step back out of the situation and imagine that their role is played by someone else. In other words put someone else in their place and then ask yourself, is that acceptable?

Now that you have a deeper understanding of the situation you should use this exercise to really look at what is going on in your relationship and also what is going on within yourself. Looking from the outside in is easier to do because you do not let the excuses and barriers get in the way. It is the best way to get a good honest look at things.

There are things that you can do, and the first place to start making changes is to yourself. That is the one thing that you do have some control over, even if you have previously surrendered that control, you can get that back by simply thinking in different terms and coming to realise that as a person you deserve more than you have. This is where we start using the pride to rebuild the self-respect and the dignity in order to become strong enough to do something about it all.

The other important thing to do in the early stages is to put the blame where it lies, and that is with the abuser. You need to stop blaming yourself for creating this situation and allowing it to continue and to get to this point. That is negative thinking and it must be stopped.

You have enough trouble fending off the attacks of the abuser, the last thing you need is negative thinking and beating yourself down by blaming yourself for all the problems that you have.

You have to remember that the abuser is the one that has created this situation and at the same time has led you down the path that you are currently on. Throughout all of this you have suffered mental and emotional abuse and to be honest I think you should be applauding yourself for hanging in there this long and trying to live a life despite the abuse.

There is no shame in being a victim in an abusive relationship, absolutely none at all, if there is any shame then it is the abuser that should be ashamed, not you.

I hope that you will use some of the things that I have talked of here to start seeing a different angle on things, and I hope that it will at least help fan the spark that I know you have inside of you. I hope the spark will ultimately shine through and allow you to break free of the torment and get on with living the life that every person on this planet deserves and that is a chance to be who you are and be free from pain and suffering.

Just before I bring this chapter to a close there is one key question that I want everyone who is reading this book to ask themselves, and to be honest when they are answering it.

Is this the way you want to spend the rest of your life?

Think about what that question means, and think about the conveyer belt that you are on. Where is it taking you?

END OF SECTION

This is the end of the section that is specifically about the victims; however it is not the end of the book. There are still lots of things that I want to talk about.

I hope that by the time that you reach this point that you have a different understanding and maybe a completely new perspective of what really goes on inside the victim in an abusive relationship and it has enlightened you enough to see that it is not just a question of packing up their things and leaving. I am sure if it were that easy then we would not have a problem with this scenario in the world today.

Throughout this section and indeed throughout the book I have talked about the victims as people that should be applauded for the strength of character that they display and how strong they have to be to get out. By now you should have a much better understanding of why I think this. Domestic abuse is much more than violence, and it is even much more than verbal and mental abuse. There are so many things going on and so many different ways that an abuser dominates the victim that it is not surprising really that the victims do stay.

Apart from the abuse and torment that the abuser is throwing at them, there is the pressure that they put on themselves. The biggest pressure that we as people have is the pressure we put on ourselves. I am sure that anyone reading this will have at least at some point put a huge amount of pressure on themselves and suffered because of it.

It is important that I once again remind you that the information that is provided here is written in general terms and will not fit all of the people and all of the relationships. It is provided as a means of prompting you to think about what is going on; if you can relate to the information that is here, even better.

It is my hope that as you have been reading through this section that at the very least it has made you think about things, maybe even for the first time. To be honest some of the ideas and concepts have even made me think a lot about things going on in my life.

I am not in an abusive relationship, but there is a lot of information in the pages of this book that apply as much to everyone's life as they do to those in domestic abuse.

Now that we have more or less covered the victim part of this book fairly comprehensively, I now want to talk about the abusers. Whether you like it or not there are two people involved in the relationship and we must look at these issues from the point of view of the abuser also.

To The Abuser

The previous section about the victim was directed to a wider audience and not specifically only for the victim. In this section I am going to be aiming this directly at the abuser. I am doing this because I do not have a full understanding of what is going on in their minds as I do with the victim.

I think that it is still important for everyone to read this section, and not just abusers. To be honest I am not sure that you will find too many people that are abusing their partners who would be interested in reading a book like this, but I am going to write it nonetheless because I think it also provides information and therefore will provoke thought for the reader.

Any information about domestic abuse can only be a good thing. It is information and understanding that helps people to think right and most importantly gives them the correct perspective on things.

It does take an abuser for there to be a victim in a relationship; I think that in fairness we should not automatically leap to the conclusion that the abusers are doing what they are because they are nasty and evil, I am sure there are those that are like that, but I do not think we can apply that to everyone.

Having said all of that we shall now move on and look into what is going on in the mind of the abusers and then we will look a little more at what someone on the outside can do to help.

DO YOU KNOW WHAT YOU ARE DOING?

I know this may sound like a strange question, but it is not always obvious to someone exactly what they are doing and therefore the consequences of those actions.

As you will have learned from the earlier sections of this book it is not always obvious when a relationship becomes abusive and a lot of it depends on the people and personalities that are involved. Just as it is fair to say that the victim does not always recognise when there is abuse it is fair to say that the same is applicable to the abuse. So the first question to the abuser has to be to ask whether they realise what they are doing and to what degree.

It is one thing to be a dominant person in a relationship but it is a different story when the dominance gets to the point where you are controlling your partner. Even if you are in control you need to really consider whether you are using that control fairly and most importantly if you are using it with respect for your partner. I would go so far as to say that when you are making decisions and choices you should be thinking about your partner and their needs and desires before you think about what you want and need.

That is what a relationship is all about, thinking about the other person before you think about yourself, that is what love is all about.

There is a very old saying that goes something like this "power corrupts; absolute power corrupts absolutely"

What that means is that when someone is in control it is very easy to become selfish and self serving with that control. It then goes on to say that the more power you have the more likely you are to take advantage of that power.

There is another saying that I prefer to use and that goes "with great power comes great responsibility".

What this means is that when you are in control and you do

have power then it is your responsibility to use that power in a proper and right fashion.

The best way for someone to test whether they are doing the right thing or not is to put themselves in the other person's position and ask themselves if they would like to be treated in the manner that they are treating their partner. What if the roles were completely reversed, how would the abuser, now the victim, think and feel about what is going on?

The next step in that scenario is then to ask would the abuser allow themselves to be treated the way that they are treating their partner?

If you honestly can do those two exercises and come to the conclusion that you would not like it and you would not allow it, do not excuse yourself or justify your actions by saying that the other person is different etc. Be honest and face up to what is going on and stop what is going on before it gathers momentum and gets worse.

Really all I can achieve with this chapter is essentially raise the point and hope that someone reading this will take a step back and think about what is going on, and maybe for the first time realise that they may not be doing the right thing in their relationship.

HOW CAN YOU MISTREAT SOMEONE YOU LOVE?

This is one of those questions that just simply continues to baffle me. The truth is, I simply have not even the slightest clue as to how someone can mistreat someone they love and have chosen as their partner for the long term.

I understand the concept of tough love and I understand there are times when we do need to be hard on people in order for them to learn and grow, but I have never understood how someone can be outright mean and nasty to anyone, let alone someone that they are in love with.

I can stretch my understanding and allow for the fact that is not always intentional in the early stages, and it can sort of develop a life of its own and can just sort of get out of control, but at some point there has to be a time when the abuser looks at what they are doing and finds that they do not like it. Or at the very least realise that they are no longer in love with the other person.

Having said that it is fair to say that as with all things in this life abuse too happens in a conveyer belt type effect and it just becomes part of the normal life, and before either party knows it, that is where things are.

I do not offer this by way of excuse, nor do I want to change the whole premise that this book is not designed to be judgemental, and I do not want to start passing judgements on anyone here.

It seems to me that at some point the abuser stopped loving the victim. The victim that they have created is no longer the person that they fell in love with. I think it would even be fair to say that just as a victim does not imagine that things are going to turn out like this in the beginning of the relationship, then the abuser does not think that things are going to turn out like they have either.

But it still remains a mystery to me how someone can mistreat a person that they love and have chosen to be a partner going forward in their life.

I think in all fairness here we have to look at all of this a little more deeply from the perspective of the abuser and perhaps try and develop a little more understanding as we go forward.

I do hope that at some point throughout this book that you really start to see what you are doing and what is going on in your relationship and your life, and I really do hope that you see that things are simply not right and that you do something about it; and I hope that it is sooner rather than later.

WHERE DOES IT START?

There are generally two different ways that being abusive starts. Firstly it comes from the preconceived ideas that the abuser has brought into the relationship. These are the things that they have learned growing up and bring as part of the baggage into the relationship.

Although the abuser does not see this as abuse, and it may not seem like it at first, it is something that is there from the very beginning and will generally escalate through time. Often it is these things that are dismissed in the early part of the relationship by both parties as just being part of it. From the victim's point of view it is just the way the abuser is, just one of those things that they have every intention of changing and fixing over time.

From the abusers point of view there is nothing wrong with it. That is how they are supposed to behave in the relationship, and the victim simply should be taking on their role, after all that is just the way that it is meant to be.

Generally speaking this first comes across as someone who is very dominant. A dominant person will generally seek out someone who is less dominant, as it then fits in with their side of the relationship. In this scenario the abuse starts out right in the very beginning. Then this becomes the norm for the relationship and will generally just get worse. If you think about this scenario in terms of the conveyer belt that we have spoken of, and then both parties in this relationship are starting out on the conveyer belt with the beginnings of an abusive relationship in place, it is only going to lead on from there and get worse.

The second example of how the abuse starts is when it develops over a period of time. This generally will not even begin until the relationship is about a year to two years old. That is when the honeymoon period is starting to wear off and the normal day to day of life starts coming into picture. This is when both parties are now living in a different reality to the one that the relationship was formed and has grown in. This is where the frustrations and all the little things in life starting getting in the way, after the rose coloured glasses have been removed and reality starts setting in.

What happens here is that generally the abuser will start being more dominant and angry. All of the things that have bothered them in the past, that they once dismissed, now starting coming out. From here the abuser will start asserting control over the victim and this is when the abuse starts coming in full swing.

It is important to note that in both of these situations that the abuse is not necessarily intentional. It could be that neither the abuser nor the victim sees what is really going on, but before they know it they are on this path.

If you think you may be abusing your partner by some of the things that you say and do, even if it is only in arguments or at times with angry outbursts, you still need to think about what is going on and maybe realise what is going on and break the cycle that is either in place or that you are most definitely heading towards.

I have to say that just because the abuser is in control; does not mean that they are happy. Think about when you chose your partner; you were not looking for a slave or someone you would abuse. You were looking for someone you would fall in love with and plan to spend the rest of your life with. Being an abuser is not a happy place to be, and bringing abuse into a relationship, through any means and at any time, does not mean that you are getting what you want. It is a fact that someone who is angry and nasty all the time simply cannot be happy.

Think about that a little.

WHERE DOES IT END?

Well that really comes down to you. At some point the victim may or may not summon the strength to break free of your grasp, so ultimately the only other way that the abuse is going to end is when you, the abuser decide to do something about it.

One of the things with abuse is that it almost becomes a habit, much the same as it does to be a victim. At some point it just becomes the normal day to day. It may start small and then sort of gather a life of its own, but that does not mean that it is OK.

An abuser by the very nature of the things is the one that it is in control. Therefore it follows that if the abuser is not happy with the way that things are then they should be the one to hold up their hand and put a stop to it. As I mentioned previously, with great power comes great responsibility. As the abuser; it is your responsibility to do something about it.

You cannot keep making excuses and blaming the victim for not living up to your expectations. If you are not happy with the victim, then do something about it. Take action to make the change; do not think that by abusing them that you are helping them to become better people, or teaching them something. You are not.

You are in essence destroying at least two lives by not doing something about it. If there are children, then it is more than two. It is not only the victim that is unhappy, and miserable, there can be no way that you are happy with the way that things are and the way that the relationship is going. I am sure that this is not the way that you thought things would work out.

Even though you are the abuser and are in control, the same things that I have spoken about throughout this book apply to you in the same way. There are still fears, excuses and barriers.

Just because you are the dominant person in the relationship does not mean that you need to take advantage of that dominance, it means that you need to take the responsibility that comes with that role and treat those around you with respect and love, and who knows it just may be reciprocated. After all you did choose to be together, but not under these circumstances.

Please think about the things that I have written here. If you are an abuser and are reading this, then you are reading it for a reason, and that is because you are not happy with your life and the way that things are not working out.

The same exercise I mentioned earlier can be used in this situation for you as well. Put yourself in the victim's position and imagine how you would like it if someone treated you in that way. Imagine that you did not want to come home because you were going to encounter a barrage of physical and mental abuse. It is not a pretty picture when you start looking at it in that way is it?

You might be saying that the victim should put themselves in your shoes and see all the things that you have to put up with. We all have things in our lives that we do not like, but we are also all responsible for what we do about it. Mistreating someone just because they do not make you happy is not the way to go about making things better. In fact it simply makes it worse. Either stop the abuse and change the relationship, or walk away.

Don't try and kid yourself that it will get better as soon as the victim changes, as soon as your job changes, as soon as the money worries go, once the kids grow up. These are all just excuses and barriers. It will get better when you do something to make it better. Either change your attitude and way of doing things, or change your address. That is the way that things will get better, not through excuses, lies and barriers.

EXCUSES, EXCUSES, EXCUSES

Just today I read a report about some council workers who got fired because they were spending two hours a day browsing the internet instead of working. The union's take on this was that it is the employer's fault for providing them with internet access and therefore creating the temptation.

In my view that is complete nonsense and is just another example of how society and people in general are very willing to do and say just about anything so that they do not have to take responsibility for the things that they do.

All that does is allow us as people to justify the things that we do, without ever having to admit the fact that we got it wrong, did it wrong, or that we are responsible anything in the way of saying 'It's my fault'.

In the case of domestic abuse it is easy for the abuser to justify the things that they do and the way that they treat their partners and that is by way of excusing their behaviour and blaming everybody else except themselves for what they do.

There are many excuses that an abuser will use, it can be anything from 'it was the way that I was bought up', or 'I am so frustrated with work, life, no money' and all that kind of thing.

These days we even have medical excuses for all this called ADD, ADHD and the like.

Then there is always the one of blaming the victim, blaming the government, blaming the education system, because you cannot get a decent job. All of these things basically make you angry and frustrated and you just need to let your anger out somehow and it is unfortunate that the one that you love is the one that suffers.

People seem to think that anger is something that needs to be released otherwise if it is bottled up it will have serious consequences for the individual. I am not sure where this myth comes from, but it truly is that, a myth.

Anger is an emotion, just like any of the others. You never hear that someone had to let their sadness out, or they had to let their love out otherwise they were going to explode. And the reality is that anger is no different. It is still an emotion that you can, and quite honestly should, learn to control.

Being angry does not give you the right to mistreat someone. It does not give you the right to abuse someone physically, mentally and emotionally. In fact there is nothing that gives you the right to do that.

Have you ever heard of someone being let off from a murder simply because they were frustrated and angry? In fact it would be more likely that they would be locked up for murder because they were frustrated and angry and took it out on someone and killed them.

At some point it could be that you are following the example set by your parents. Whilst this is true to some degree, there has to come a point when you become an adult and have to take responsibility for who you are and what you do. There are many examples of the right way to behave in a relationship, and there really is no genuine basis or excuse to blame your parents for the way that you behave.

I could cite a whole heap of excuses, and I am sure that sooner or later I would get to the one that you like to use, but that is not the point I am trying to make here. The point that I am trying to make is that there is not a good enough excuse to justify what you are doing to your partner.

If you think you do have a valid reason for what you are doing, then I would love to hear from you. Please email me at brian@smellthereality.com

Ultimately it is up to the abuser to stand up and take responsibility for what they are doing and do something about it.

OLD FASHIONED IS NOT AN EXCUSE

Although I did say that I was not going to talk about all of the individual excuses that could come out, there are a couple that I do want to address directly and this is one of them.

It seems to be that because a couple are behaving in what was once a stereotypical way, and that is; with the man in charge and the woman being subservient, then this is a great way to excuse being a bully and a nasty person. It is not a good enough reason as far as I am concerned.

This is used as almost a throw away excuse for someone being a bully, and generally in this case it is the male. I know I said that it is not always the male and that I will try and keep any sort of gender bias out of this, but in this particular instance I think it is justified that in the case of someone being old fashioned and this being used as an excuse for abuse, then more often than not it is aimed at the male.

Let me give you a little insight into the old fashioned way and how it relates to relationships today, and how someone who is using that tag is using it as an excuse to dominate, control and in effect abuse the other person.

To do this we are going to have a bit of a history lesson. In the days gone past, relationships and in fact society was based on a very different premise to what it is based on in today.

I am sure that everyone has heard the expression "Rule of Thumb". There is very popular and wide belief that this came from a law that stated that a man was able to beat his wife with a stick, as long as it was no thicker than his thumb, hence the "Rule of Thumb".

Research suggests that this not actually true, however the fact that a lot of people believe this to be true shows that they believe that the attitudes to relationships, going back in the past clearly show that it was very male dominated.

If you have a look back fifty or sixty years ago when our

grandparents were starting out in their relationship, it was very much a male dominated world. This was then carried into the relationship and the home and therefore the home was also very much male dominated.

It is this environment that our parents were raised in and this is where they learned their ideas about relationships and how things should be done. So the premise that the man is in charge in the home has carried on through time. It is only our generation that has truly come to look upon all people as being equal, and therefore created equality throughout relationships and the home.

This is not something that is universal, and will more than likely take another two or three generations before it is truly accepted as being the norm.

In the 70's it was acceptable and normal for the man to be the king in the home. After all it was always said that a man's home is his castle. But now in 2007, this is simply not the case anymore.

In modern times, this stereotyping has well and truly gone out of the window and someone using this as an excuse, to abuse the victim is either living in the dark ages, or simply trying to hide from the truth.

Even in the days gone by, when the man was the automatic ruler in the home it still came with a degree of respect, love and understanding for their partner. When it didn't, then it was still an abusive relationship, whether it was deemed to be acceptable or not.

Old Fashioned is not a valid reason for mistreating someone; it is simply an excuse and in this day and age a very bad one at that.

IT IS NOT THE VICTIM'S FAULT

It is very easy for the abuser to blame the victim for making them do the things that they do. I keep going on about this point, because I think it is very important for everyone to accept responsibility for the things that they do at all times.

In an abusive relationship the abuser is the one who is responsible for creating and continuing the abuse, but it is unlikely that they are going to put their hand up and admit that they have been nasty, and horrible to the person that they love and in the interest of the other person, they are going to leave. I am sure that it does happen at times, but it is rare.

The more likely scenario is that the abuser will think they are doing nothing wrong, they are completely within their rights to do what they are doing.

To blame the victim for the way that you are treating them is simply being a coward. That is a bit harsh, but when it comes down to it is true. How can you blame someone that you have made a victim; and have abused at least mentally and emotionally, controlled and made to live in fear, for making you do it? It is simply does not make sense.

Perhaps there are many valid reasons why you are angry, frustrated and quite possibly do not like your partner anymore, but that is not a valid reason for treating them in this way, and it is certainly not their fault that all the things in your world are not working out.

You may not even think that it is abuse, but you have to control your victim because they are unable to do it for themselves and you are unable to trust them. Once again, if there is no trust in the relationship then perhaps it is time to walk away from it. That is a better option than controlling and dominating your partner and forcing them to be the person that you want them to be.

Ultimately what you are doing, you are doing for whatever

reason you want to tell yourself in order to justify it, but do not think that there is any valid way of justifying mistreating another person. You certainly cannot justify blaming the victim for what you do. They are just trying to survive the pain and torment that you are putting them through, how can they possibly be to blame for that?

You simply cannot blame them for that. So if you don't like them and you don't trust them, then surely the thing to do would be to work on the relationship to reconcile your differences or bring the relationship to an end.

You would not like someone trying to change the person that you are just because they did not like you, why would you think that it is OK for you to do it to someone else?

I hope that by now you are starting to see a little sense and you are looking into what is going on here. There are so many better ways to be living your life, than spending your time abusing another person.

WHAT ABOUT THE KIDS

I talked earlier about how the kids are affected in an environment of abuse. I want to raise it again here, specifically targeted at the abuser and ask them what do they think they are teaching the children by continuing to behave the way that they are and continuing to demonstrate that it is not only OK to be an abuser, it is also OK to be a victim.

You know your kids are going to grow up to be adults and they are going to go into relationships and they are going to take all of the things that you teaching them now with them. Apart from all of that, can you imagine what they are going through right now.

Whether you believe it or not, a home that is based on an abusive relationship is most certainly not a happy home. There is no way that it can be. It is not happy for you and it is not happy for the victim but most importantly it is not a happy home for the children.

When your kids grow up and they look back on their childhood, what are the things that are going to stick out in their memories? How are they going to regard you in years to come?

Are they going to look back at this time in their lives, the time when they should be care free and happy, learning and growing, are they going to be thinking about you as a person that they admired and looked up to, or are they going to be thinking of you as the person who was always angry and nasty to the other parent. Bullying and putting the other down and creating an environment of fear, anger and resentment?

I am sure that you have realised by now that there is so much going on that goes far beyond just the interaction between you and your partner. If there are kids involved, there is simply no way you can justify the environment that you are creating for them to live in.

It is you that is creating it. Not the victim, not the bad job you have, not the lack of money or any of the other things you like to blame. When your kids look back with disdain upon the world you created for them as children, it is not going to be pleasant for you.

You are responsible for what you do now, you are responsible for what you teach your children, and ultimately you are responsible for the type of adults they are going to become.

Once again you are the dominant one and you are the one that is in control, you blame the victim for being a bad parent and all the other things, but you cannot be a good parent and be abusing your partner at the same time. It is not possible. Your kids will grow to dislike you and to even hate you. If you are lucky they will come to pity you, but if you keep doing what you are doing then you really cannot expect to get anything else from them.

No! It is not your right

We have touched on this throughout this book but I wanted to include this chapter because it is a very simple and important message and I do not want it to be missed.

It is not your right to be able to control and abuse your partner. There is no reason why you should think that you have that position in the relationship. You do not have that position within society, and it is no different in the home.

There is no reason why one person in the relationship should be of lesser value than the other person, and there is no reason why one person should dominate another or think they are more important or superior to the other person.

Whatever you think about all of the other things that I have spoken of in this book and whatever you may think of yourself and your relationship, you need to know this for a fact. You do not have a right in any way, to dominate or control another person against their will.

If you get nothing else from this book, then understand this plain and simple fact. It is not your right to abuse your partner!

IF YOU DON'T LIKE THE VICTIM, WHY DON'T YOU LEAVE?

We talked about the victims and why they stay in an abusive relationship, these apply to the abuser as well. You are obviously not happy with your partner even though you have all of the control and the power, yet you choose to keep the abuse going, and do nothing about it. It just does not seem to add up to me. Surely this is not the type of relationship that you wanted in the beginning.

When you were standing at the altar, all loved up and making the vows together; this is not what you had in mind. You may say that your partner has not lived up to their end of the arrangement either, and that may well be true, but that does not mean that you have to stay around just to abuse them.

I understand that you might be experiencing many frustrations and or fears that we have spoken about throughout this book and you may also have excuses and barriers, but you have to think that if the relationship is not working out, perhaps everyone would simply be better off if you were to leave.

Your partner is not your possession, it is not about giving up something that you own, it is about being a reasonable human being and seeing that what you are doing is simply not working out.

It is not only the victim that is suffering; it is also not working out for you. You can't tell me that to come home to a place where you are not loved, or even liked is something that you look forward to at the end of the day.

If you do not want to leave, at least enable the victim to leave and try doing the right thing. As the leader of the household you need to take responsibility for it and for all of the people in it. At least be big enough to make it so that both of you and the children, if there are any, are able to get out of the relationship and move on with their lives.

Not just for the sake of the victim, but for the children, and most importantly for you. You have a right to a happy life, but you do not have a right to abuse someone else, so why not make the choices that will enable you to have a happy life. It may mean that you have to face a few things about yourself, and it may feel like you are losing out, but this is not a situation that you can win.

You are never going to create the relationship that you wanted by creating a victim who lives in a state of mental and emotional abuse. You are never going to get back what you have taken away from the victim and you are never going to be happy again, if you keep doing what you are doing.

A relationship is not the place where you win or lose. Even as an abuser in this relationship you are losing. You may think that it is the victim that is losing, but you are also losing out. You are losing out on the opportunity to live the sort of life and have the sort of relationship that you wanted when it all started.

Maybe you need to simply cut your losses and bring the relationship to end, if not for the victim and the children, but for your own sake.

WHAT DO YOU TELL YOUR FRIENDS?

Here is something for you to think about. When you are with your friends and you are chatting about things at home are you happy to be honest with your friends and tell them what it is really like and what really goes on?

If you answer no to that question then you have to sort of wonder why you aren't honest about it. The obvious answer to that is that you are ashamed and embarrassed by what goes on in your home.

For you to be embarrassed about it that means that you know that what you are doing is wrong. You don't tell them because you know they will judge you for it and you don't want people to know what you are really like.

If you know that it is wrong, and you are ashamed to talk about it, then why do you keep doing it? Why can't you admit to yourself that you are not happy and that you want it to change?

Considering the abuser is usually the dominant person and full of their own importance this all sounds like a very cowardly thing to be doing. Too scared to admit what you are doing is wrong to your friends and too cowardly to do anything about stopping it from happening.

WHERE HAS THE RESPECT AND LOVE GONE?

You know it is not only the victim that has lost the love and the respect, it is also the abuser. In order to treat someone like this and abuse them demonstrates on many levels that there is no love and respect for the other person.

It may be that the love and respect went out of the relationship a long time ago and it was replaced by anger and resentment which has led to the abuse and the current environment.

I am sure that you try and tell yourself that you love and respect the victim, and I am sure that you try and tell yourself that they also love and respect you, but that is simply not true.

There is no way that love and respect can exist in this environment. The victim may try and tell themselves that they still love the abuser, but ultimately it is not true. The things that the relationship was created on, namely love, respect, honour and friendship are long gone. What they have been replaced with are anger, fear, frustration, resentment, dislike and misery. They are the things that are now the foundation of the relationship.

If you think any differently then you are not being honest about the whole thing. If you do not believe me then take a few minutes to think about the whole picture and see for yourself.

Think about how it all was in the beginning, and the good times that you had together. Think about how it used to feel when you were together. Think about how you used to treat your partner and how they used to treat you.

Now think about how it is now. There is no doubt that relationships change. Once the courting and things settle into the day to day, but this goes beyond that. If you are still not seeing the picture, compare your current relationship to the relationships that you see your friends and family having. How does it measure up?

I suggest that it does not measure up very well at all. In fact I am sure that if you do this properly and you are honest with yourself about it, it is quite obvious the way things have turned out.

This book is all about thinking about what is really going in your life and going beyond the day to day struggle, and seeing what is going on beneath the surface. You have to see that the relationship is not working and there is no love and respect there; from either side.

If there are children involved then you should also be asking yourself if there is any love and respect there, or is it simply that you force them to behave in a certain way?

Love and respect is something that you earn in the first place and it is something that you need to keep earning along the way. It is not an award that no one can take away from you. It is something that is given where it is deserved and not demanded.

It does not come with position or title, it comes because you do the things that make you the sort of person that deserves to be loved and respected, not because you create an environment of anger and fear and force people to treat you in the way that you feel you are entitled to.

Once again all I ask is that you think about the things that are written here and take them on board. And always keep in mind that love and respect is also a two way street. You cannot demand from others what you do not give out yourself. Abusing someone; is not loving and it is not respectful.

WHERE IS IT GOING, ON THE CURRENT COURSE?

Here is something else to think about, it is another important part of the whole picture. Given that we have already spoken about the fact that you cannot be happy with the way things are; don't forget that we are being honest here; then the next step is to take the current situation and think about what it is going to be like in five years time.

Try and be as honest as you can when you are doing this. Given the current situation in the relationship, where you are with it, where your partner is with it, and if there are kids involved where they are with it; then try and think forward; given the current course that you are on, where is this leading you to?

When you have done this, compare it to the way you thought things were going to be when you started the relationship.

I am sure that you are seeing a very different picture. It goes far beyond what we all imagine in the beginning and ideal images we have of our life together, and then the reality sets in, it is not a very pretty picture, and I am sure that you are thinking about the better side of things and not the worse case scenario.

Right back at the beginning of this book I talked about Ange and her relationship, do you think that her ex-husband imagined when things started out that he would end up serving five years in prison for raping her? Do you think he set out to mistreat and abuse her for fifteen years? I can tell you that he did not, but that is what he did, and now he is paying the price for it.

I am not suggesting that you are as bad as he is or anything like that, but I am telling you that there will be a price to pay for abusing your partner. It may not be now and it may not be in the near future, but it will come.

It may come in the form of your kids looking at you with disgust and hatred. It may be that your partner will finally get the courage together to pack up and leave you. It may be that the abuse continues to escalate until it does become a police matter. It is not for me to say, it is something that you need to be thinking about.

You are on a path that you are controlling, and that path is taking you somewhere, the question is where is it taking you, and is it where you want to be heading?

That is something that only you can answer, but please take the time to go through this little exercise and be honest about it, because you may well be in control at the moment, but there will come a time when you are not going to be in control, how are you going to deal with it then?

If you are not happy with the way things are now, and you are not happy about the way that it is all going, then the good news is that you can do something about it. You may not like the things that you need to do in the short term to change things, but when it comes down to looking at the future it is better to make changes now, than it is to wait and ultimately pay the price for continuing to do what you are doing.

TIME TO TAKE RESPONSIBILITY

Throughout this section I have been talking directly to you, the abuser and I tried to get you to open your eyes and see what it is that you are doing.

By now you have either accepted the things that I have been saying and are ready to do something about it, or you have given up on all this a long time ago, because it applies to someone else, not you, or you really do believe that I am talking to you but you are still trying to deny it and you are therefore not going to do anything about it.

If you are in the category where you have accepted the things that I have spoken about then now is the time to do something about it. I do not know if you can still salvage your relationship, or whether it is simply too late and it is time to move on, that is for you and your partner to decide.

The key thing here is that now you have realised the fact that things need to change you must take responsibility for what has been happening and also take the responsibility for doing something about it.

The time for making excuses, laying blame, and creating barriers is now gone, and you have to look at yourself and hold your hand up and accept what has happened and then do something about it.

Even if it means that the relationship has to end and you have to go your separate ways. It has not been working out for either of you anyway, so when it comes down to it you are not really losing anything. The relationship as you wanted it and imagined it disappeared long ago, the person that you first fell in love with and planned a future together has gone.

As you are the dominant one in the relationship it is up to you to make it right. You need to keep in mind where your partner is mentally and emotionally and understand that they may not be in a position to make the right choices, after all that is what you have done to them, so take on the responsibility that you have worked so hard to gain, add some respect in there for yourself and your partner and do what needs to be done to break the cycle that you are in and step off of the conveyer belt.

I wish you all the luck in the world if you are ready to do this. I am willing to help if you are genuine in what you want to do, then please get in touch.

THE GUY IN THE GLASS

Following is a Poem that was written by Dale Wimbrow in around 1934 and I think that it is as relevant today as it has ever been. Although I am including this in the abuser section, I think it something that everyone needs reminding of at times.

I am presenting here in honour of Dale Wimbrow, in its original format.

The Guy in the Glass
by Dale Wimbrow, (c) 1934

When you get what you want in your struggle for pelf,
And the world makes you King for a day,
Then go to the mirror and look at yourself,
And see what that guy has to say.

For it isn't your Father, or Mother, or Wife,
Who judgement upon you must pass.
The feller whose verdict counts most in your life
Is the guy staring back from the glass.

He's the feller to please, never mind all the rest,
For he's with you clear up to the end,
And you've passed your most dangerous, difficult test
If the guy in the glass is your friend.

You may be like Jack Horner and "chisel" a plum,
And think you're a wonderful guy,
But the man in the glass says you're only a bum
If you can't look him straight in the eye.

You can fool the whole world down the pathway of years,
And get pats on the back as you pass,
But your final reward will be heartaches and tears
If you've cheated the guy in the glass.

END OF SECTION

It is generally the first reaction to point and blame the abuser, and to be honest I must say that I have very little compassion for them, but at the same time I understand that an abusive relationship is not always a deliberate thing.

I understand that just as being a victim is something that can creep up on you, so too, can being an abuser. It does not mean that you are a bad person all the time, it just means that you have been caught up in it all, and sometimes you need help to break the cycle.

Do not feel that there is nowhere that you can go to get help. There are many organisations that will help the abuser; it is not always about the victim. Provided you are genuine in your realisations and you are ready to make a change; then there is help, there is hope and there is a way.

There are two key things that you need to do to benefit from the help available. Firstly you have to admit that you do have problems at home and that you are willing to do something about it. The second thing is that you need to actually do something about it and seek the help that is available.

As I said, I am willing to help and you can get in touch with me, or one of the many other organisations out there.

I wish you luck, and I do hope that you will learn and grow throughout all the experiences and make sure that it is not something that you allow to happen again.

HOW YOU CAN HELP

*T*his section is aimed at those that are on the outside and looking in. Generally these are the people who are at the very least a little more objective about things and see a little more clearly what is happening.

Although this is not aimed at the victim or the abuser, it is still worthwhile reading as there is still information here that you may find useful. If you are honest, you are reading this book hoping that it will ignite something in you or give you something to hold onto and help you to sort things out. You never know it may just be in this section.

Although this chapter is called 'How you can help', I must stress once again that I am not able to provide you a step by step guide here. I do not know enough about the individual situation and the people and personalities involved to be able to do that. Ange and I can help on a one on one basis if that is what you are looking for and you can contact either of us through the website (www.smellthereality.com), this applies to victims, abusers and those who are trying to help. However in this book what I do want to provide you with are ideas and insights that hopefully will assist you in what you are trying to do. Once again it is the principles and ideas that are important, and what they come to mean to you in your situation, not the way that I write them, and not so much in a literal translation.

I am dealing more with helping the victim rather than the abuser in the following sections. If you are trying to help an abuser to see what they are doing is wrong and are failing in your efforts, perhaps you should turn your attention to start helping the victim to get them out of the relationship.

Take what you read here, think about it in reference to the situation you are trying to deal with and go from there.

So this section is designed to try and help someone who is trying to help someone that is stuck in an abusive relationship, whether they know it or not. Throughout this book I have made reference to things that you need to keep in mind, but it is here that I hope to provide some of the key ideas and pointers that will hopefully help you to help someone else.

BEING A FRIEND

The best and perhaps the easiest thing that you can do for someone who is stuck in an abusive relationship is to simply be a friend. Although this is easy for me to say here, it may not be as easy as it sounds in the real world.

There are many things that can come between friends when one of them is a victim. It can be like walking on eggshells at times to be around someone who you know is being victimised without being able to even say anything about it.

One of the key things to keep in mind is that isolation is one of the tools that the abuser uses in their quest for control and dominance, and it is vital that you do what you have to in order to make sure that the friendship remains.

That may even mean having to spend time with someone whom you know is abusing your friend. This can be especially difficult to do, but try and keep in mind that it is because of your friend and your friendship that you must go through these things.

Sometimes I think it is harder to sit by and watch anyone being abused, and harder still when it is someone that you know and love, but you have to be aware that the victim is being put through enough within their relationship and do not need to get hassle from anyone else. The key to it is not to push too hard when the victim is not ready to see the real situation. If the victim is not open to be helped then there is nothing more that you can do except to be a friend and help them the best that you can, without putting pressure on your friendship.

Friends are people that are there through the good times and the bad times. When someone is having a bad time that is when they need someone just to be a friend. They do not need to know how hard it is for you to watch them going through this, they do not need to know that you are not sure that you can sit back and do nothing, they do not need to know that you can't stand their partner and you will have nothing to do with them. At some point you have to think in terms of the victim you are trying to help, and just let some things run their course, and not put up barriers that will hinder them from receiving your help.

The most important thing is to make sure that the friendship remains, even though it may make you angry and frustrated at times, it is important that you get through this stage, without putting pressure on the victim; they have enough to deal with already. They do not need to know that what they are doing is upsetting you. This will also create distance and add to the isolation.

The essence of it is that you can only help if the friendship is in tact when the victim is ready to receive help. If you have burnt the bridges before it gets to this point, then the victim can't come to you for help.

UNDERSTAND WHAT IS REALLY HAPPENING

Reading a book like this will give you some understanding of what is happening below the surface but the understanding that you need to develop goes beyond the general and has to get into the specifics.

Earlier in this book there was a chapter called 'behind closed doors'. In this chapter I talked about the fact that nobody knows what goes on behind closed doors and things can be very different to what you know or what you think you know.

What you have to do as an outsider is to try and understand what is going on specifically, this means that you cannot rely on all the things that the victim is telling you. There are a couple of reasons for this.

Firstly the victim will not be honest about what is happening. We have already discussed this in terms of how they will not be honest about how bad things are earlier, but the other side of it is that perhaps the victim is making out it is worse than it is. I know that does not sound very friendly, but it is not unheard of that some people like to act the victim, and make things out to be a lot worse than they really are.

Once again, I am not making any judgements on anyone here, I am trying to provide information that you can take on to help you deal with the situation.

Some people use the victim status as a means of drawing attention to themselves, and sometimes this is not even a conscious thing, it is just something that they do.

The point is; you need to make sure you understand as much as you can about what is ACTUALLY happening so that when the time is right, you are in a position to help.

As in most things, knowledge and understanding can only be a help, and this is certainly no different. In fact I think it would be fair to say that it is essential that you gain as much understanding and knowledge about the situation as you can.

It is not only the situation that is important, it is also critical that you also understand the people that are involved. The more you know the better equipped you are to help.

DON'T PUSH TOO HARD

If there is one thing that a victim does not need; it is more pressure from other people. When you try to push too hard, then all you do is create extra stress and pressure on the victim.

Remember when you are helping someone in an abusive relationship, chances are they are not at their best, so increasing the pressure on them will simply do more harm than good.

As you have read the victim will go through stages of denial and hope, and during these times there is nothing that you can say or do that will change their mind and help them to see what is happening. It is only when they are ready to see that there is a problem that it will come out, until then you have to be very careful about what you say and how you say it.

One of the critical things that you must never do in this situation is to give them an ultimatum. There is nothing that they want more in life than to make their relationship work and there is nothing that will entice them away from it.

It is only when the denial and hope are gone that the victim even comes to believe that they have a problem. It does not mean that they will admit it to you, so you are still a little stuck in terms of what you can do. The problem you have is that once the denial and hope stages are over that is when all the fears start becoming very real.

By this time the self-respect and dignity is down, so it is likely that they do not think that they need help and they are getting all that they deserve, even if they weren't at that point; then the fear is the thing that is stopping them from doing anything.

You may think that as you read through this that I am telling you that there is never a good time to push hard with the victim, and to a point that is true. Again I have to reinforce that I am talking generally and each specific situation is different.

You will find that if you are trying to help a victim there is only one way that you can do it, at least to begin with, and that is very gently and almost subtly. A sledge hammer will not work, but it does not mean that you can't tap away very gently and over a period of time to make a big difference.

When I say that you have to do it almost subtly, I am talking about how you sort of drop things into a conversation and not make a big deal about it, but do what I like to call plant the seed.

This is where you tell them something that they will think about a bit later and hopefully arrive at the conclusion that you were looking for. An example of this is perhaps that you want to go and do something at the weekend, so you drop little hints throughout the week, and by the time the weekend comes round you and your partner are on the same page, because you have been preparing them all week, and they are happy to do it, because they believe they have thought of it for themselves.

This is a useful way to help the victim, without confronting them, and without making them defensive.

In interpersonal relationships we know that as soon as someone attacks, then the person being attacked becomes defensive, it is an automatic response. If you say to the victim that they are being mistreated and their partner is nasty and the whole thing is not right, then in a sense you are attacking the victim, even though it is not directly, but they will still feel the need and will automatically defend themselves, their partner and the situation. You have to remember that they are in a defensive mode at most times anyway, and this is how they will respond if put under pressure.

After reading this book, which you should leave laying around for them to find so that you can talk to them about it when they do find it, you now have an idea about the fears that the victim is going through. They will never tell you that they are afraid of these things, they may not even have thought about it directly, but it is there in the back of their mind, so you need to also chip away at the fears.

The biggest thing that you need to do is keep reminding them that they are worthy people and they do deserve to have all of the good things in life. Try and build their self-respect and dignity. It is ultimately this that is going to get them to the point where they can do something about it.

If you do want to talk to them about domestic abuse, apart from leaving this book around for them to find, then make it about someone else, not the victim. The old 'I have a friend who…' trick. It is another way that will work, because what you are doing is talking about the issue and not directing it at them and therefore you are not attacking them. This is another way of planting the seed; it will give them something to think about.

Do not go in with a sledge hammer and guns blazing, it will put pressure on the victim and it may just destroy your relationship. Be thoughtful, careful and gentle. Keep in mind where the person is with things, and most importantly where they are with themselves.

DON'T GET INVOLVED IN THE BLAME GAME

It is very easy to take sides with the victim and start blaming their partner for everything. This may seem like a perfectly reasonable thing to do, after all they are to blame for doing what they do; and you are probably right on those things; but you have to be sensitive to the situation of the victim.

Just because a victim has an abusive partner does not mean that they don't still look on their partner as a reflection of themselves. So if you get into the blame game and start putting the partner down, you are in essence putting the victim down.

What happens then is the attack and defence scenario that I mentioned in the previous chapter. If you push hard enough then all you will end up with is the victim being backed into a corner, telling you that they still love them, and there is nothing more that you can do.

I always find that the best way to help the victim is to concentrate on the victim. The abuser is not something that you can do a lot about, but it is with the victim that you can make enough difference to enable them to do something for themselves, and bring a solution to the situation.

Talk about general unrelated situations, talk about the victim and encourage them to take the action for themselves, leave the abuser out of it and leave the blame game to them. Focus on the victim; that is where the change has to come from.

IT HAS TO COME FROM SELF AWARENESS

It does not matter how many of us try to help the victim, it does not matter how bad the abuse gets, it does not matter what the situation is; there is only one person that can really do anything about it, because it is unlikely that the abuser will, and that is the victim.

This is why domestic abuse continues in the way that it does, because it all works on a cycle whereby the victim is truly the one that needs to make the change, however they are not generally in a position to do it, and therefore it just keeps going.

Ultimately it is the victim that has to at least admit that they have a problem and then they have to find the courage to do something about it. Both of those things are very major steps for the victim, and although you can guide them and help get them to those points, they are the only ones that can actually do something about it.

As a helper it is your job to help build the person to get strong enough to almost face the abuser, if you like. It does not have to be in person, but ultimately they need to be able to say that they have had enough and are looking to move on.

It is also important to the future state of mind of the victim how they come to end the relationship. It is one thing to run and hide and live in fear, it is another thing entirely to be able to walk away with dignity and self-respect and let the abuser know that they are no longer the victim. I realise that the second scenario is not always possible, but if you think about the fact that the victim still has to lead the rest of their lives then it is important how the abuse is brought to an end.

As a helper it is not your responsibility to end the abuse, it is your responsibility to help the victim get to the point where they are mentally and emotionally able to end it for themselves. For them to want to end it they have to realise that they are being mistreated and they do deserve more than they are getting from their partner. They also need to reach the point where they are no longer willing to tolerate it, and that is when they can actually do something.

When the victim is at that point, that is when they really need the practical help to actually do something about it. Up until then you are helping the victim mentally and emotionally, and most of that will be from behind the scenes.

There are many reasons why a victim never reaches the stage where they have simply had enough and are willing and able to do something about it. Just looking in from the outside you may think they should be at that stage right now and be ready to make the move. But there are many considerations in the mind of the victim e.g. children, mortgages etc.

All of the information in this book is designed to help you to understand what is going on in the mind of the victim and why a victim may not reach this stage. When you understand what is going on you can help the victim to get to this point.

Focus on the victim, help them become the person that is able to reach the point of becoming aware that the way things are at present is not right and not only do they deserve better, there are ways to make sure that they get it. Help them to face the fears and help them to learn and grow enough to break free from the abuse, and also to make sure that they do not go back to it, and that they can move forward with their lives. They may be a victim at the moment, but they are also a lot more than that, and there is life after the abuse, and that is as important, if not more so than the current situation.

This is why I talk about focussing on the victim, not the situation and not the abuser. Ultimately it is up to the victim to take a stand and make a change.

THEY DO STILL HAVE OPTIONS

What you will notice as you read through this book and any of my other works is that one of the key things I believe in is being responsible for your actions and also being aware that in life you always have choices and options.

What happens with domestic abuse is that the abuser tries to make it seem as though the victim does not have options, and that is one of the ways that they gain control over them, by stripping them of their ability to see their options.

Options are not removed they are simply hidden away behind a veil of fear, abuse and self doubt so that the victim comes to believe that they do not have options available to them. What happens then is that they have to choose to stay where they are as they do not believe they have any other options to choose from.

In one way I am saying that a victim does choose to stay in the relationship, but at the same time I am also saying that they do not do it by choice. I know this seems a little contradictory and confusing but it is in fact true.

When we make choices, as we do all day every day, we make those choices based on the options that we have available to us. For example when you choose to buy something for lunch, the choice you make is based on a number of things, but ultimately the overriding factor is that you have to choose from the things that are available for you to buy.

I am sure that if we could we would all choose to drive expensive cars and live in big nice houses, but the truth is those options are simply not available to all of us because we do not have the money to do it, so then what we have to do is to choose from the options that we have available. We (Ange and I) choose to live in Surrey and drive a certain car, because out of the options available, they were the ones that were preferable to us.

When a victim in an abusive relationship decides to stay in the relationship they are doing it for a number of different reasons, but mostly it is because they do not have, or are not aware that they do have other options available to them. The abuser certainly does not want them to have other options, so they do what they can to make sure that even if the victim is aware that there are options, they present the options as worse than the option of staying where they are and putting up with the abuse.

Throughout this book I have spoken of fear, excuses and barriers, these are all things that do exactly the same thing, they remove options. Whether they remove options by making them worse than the current situation as with fear, or they remove options by creating reasons to justify staying in the relationship, as with excuses or they remove options by justifying why it is not a valid and realistic option as with barriers.

When I talk about a victim choosing to stay where they are, what I am saying is that through fear, excuses, barriers etc. in effect the victims cannot see their options, and therefore effectively they are left with little else to choose form.

One of the key things that a supporter can do for a victim is to let them know and continue to reinforce that no matter what they may think, or what the abuser is telling them, they do in fact have other options available to them. Whether they choose to see those options is another story altogether, but at some point they will need to know that they do have options and choices.

It may be that some of the options are not ideal, in fact it is more than likely that they are not, but part of being responsible for ourselves, is also looking at the consequences that we are creating by the choices that we make or don't make. In the short term some of the options may seem terrible, but the long term consequence is what is more important. Everything does have consequences, and it is the consequences that you have to live with, and it may not come into effect immediately, but it always will sooner or later.

What I mean by that is that although some of the options may not seem too pleasant in the short term, in the long term the difference between breaking free of the abuse can be far better than the short term hassle that may come from some of the options.

It is important to make sure that the victim does know that they do have options available to them, despite what they may think. All options have consequences, and it is not possible for me to make recommendations either way from this position.

Keep in mind that the victim will still try and work against the options using all of the things that we have talked about throughout this book, but once again it comes down to planting seeds so that when the victim is ready to do something, then they do know that they have options. It is only when you have options that you have choices, and then they can make their choices accordingly. You cannot choose something that is not an available option, so keep as many of the options open for them as possible.

SUPPORT, SUPPORT AND SUPPORT

The message in this chapter is quite simple in that if you are trying to help a victim then it is your job to simply support them; no matter what it is they choose to do. Keep in mind that there are all sorts of reasons that people make the choices that they do.

When I think of support in this instance the thing that comes to mind is to offer unconditional support. What that means to me is support that comes without judgment, and without restrictions.

It is very easy when you are sitting on the outside to judge what is happening and also judge the people that are involved. I have struggled all the way through this book to keep judgment out of it and to try and keep it open, honest and informative, without casting judgement; it is not an easy thing to do. As people one of the things that we are all good at is judging others and comparing them against ourselves and our situation.

Right back in the early sections of this book I talked about my first thought always was 'why don't they just leave?' What this is really saying is well if they don't want to leave then it is really up to them to live with the choices that they make. It is only when you move the judgments out of the way and really look at a situation in a different way, as I have tried to do here, that you come to realise that there is so much more to it than you first realised.

Even when we think what we are doing is in the best interest of the victim, we still judge the victim by how they respond to the help that we are trying to offer them. In other words the help is coming with a condition that the victim is supposed to take the help and not try and work against you.

In order to truly help the victim then you have to do it purely because you want to help the victim, and therefore you have to support them in the things that they do and the choices that they make. You may not agree with them all of the time, but I am sure that the victim believes they have a valid reason for what they do, and you may not know what that is, it may be an excuse or a barrier, but as far as the victim is concerned it is perfectly valid. There is no point holding the decision against them and withdrawing support.

As soon as you start giving ultimatums and conditions for your support or help then all you are doing is forcing the victim away, and that is the last thing that they need.

Supporting a victim in domestic abuse is very hard work. A lot of the time it is like walking on eggshells, and hitting your head against a brick wall, but that is the way it has to be done.

Ensure that your support comes without judgement and without conditions, and that the victim knows that you will support them whatever they decide to do. That is the only way that you can truly offer support and help to a victim. Judgement, conditions and criticism will only drive them away.

DON'T HELP THEM WALLOW IN THEIR MISERY

This is something that is very easy to get caught in, and it can also be very dangerous. It does not help the victim, and what essentially happens is that the relationship, between you and the person you are trying to help, becomes a pity party and does not help the situation.

You have to empathise with the victim as much as you can, but do not buy into the misery or help them wallow in it. It is OK for them to come to you and have a moan and get things off their chest, and by all means allow them to do it, but don't get caught up in it and don't allow it to dominate your relationship with them.

A victim needs somewhere where they are able to bring their problems and they need to know that you will not judge them for either doing it or for it happening in the first place, but they also need to know that you want to help them break free of it. You need to make sure that you are spending your time talking about options and all of the other things in this book, and not joining in the misery.

Always keep in mind that your aim is to bring them out of the misery, not to join them in it. This is not a case of when in Rome, this is a case where things are wrong they need to be corrected, not justified and excused, which is what you will be doing if you join in, rather than empathising and moving on.

Don't give up

One of the things that you will find is that the victim will come to rely on you to help get through the tough times they are having at home.

I know that it is a most frustrating and infuriating situation that they are living in, and you just want to grab them by the shirt and give them a good shake and hope they will wake up and see what is happening. I know that you will feel like you are not getting anywhere, I know that you will tell yourself that you can't stand to sit by and watch someone you love going through this, but you must never give up.

When a victim comes to rely on you being there for them and you give up; that just reinforces in the victim all the things that abuser is telling them. That nobody is interested in them and all of the other things that they are using to put them down.

If you become someone's 'rock' then you have to stick with it, regardless of how it is making you feel. As long as it is physically possible then you need to make sure the victim knows that you will not give up on them. It is a very big deal for the victim to be able to trust and rely on someone. Remember that their partner has betrayed them by becoming an abuser. They thought that their partner was going to be the one that was going to be there for them, care for them and look out for them. Trust becomes a very big issue for a victim, as they have been betrayed in one of the worst ways that they can, so it is critical that you hang in there.

I am not saying that you need to put your own life on hold or anything like that, but what I am saying is that as frustrating and annoying as the whole thing can get, you need to be there for the victim and they need to know that they can always come to you.

It is not a short path and it is not an easy one, but it is worth going down for someone that you love. This also follows on from not making things conditional, such as 'if you stay in that relationship, then I do not want to see you anymore, it is just too hard to watch'. That is not going to do anything other than isolate the victim even more.

Hang in there, no matter what and sooner or later you will be able to steer a victim to a better place, after all that is what you want in the first place.

SOME PRACTICAL THINGS YOU CAN DO

So far throughout this section I have been talking about things that you can do, and none of them are very specific, it has been more about providing support and guidance, however there are some specific things that you can do that will also help. Here are a few suggestions.

Keep a diary

Although we always hope that it will not become a police matter, there is always a chance that it will and the best way to help them when it does is by keeping a diary.

The sorts of things that you want to record in the diary are things like how the victim was when you saw them; this could be that they looked really tired and worn down. It could be to record physical marks and bruises or the things that they have told you that have happened.

Make sure you date every entry, and make sure that it is honest and true. Do not think to make things up to make it look worse because if the diary is needed, then it will need to be relied on as evidence and any doubt about its truthfulness will mean that the whole thing is worthless.

Do not tell the victim that you are keeping this, they will stop telling you things to help protect the abuser, and do not use it against the victim when you are telling them that they need to do something about it. It is not something to get out and show the victim how bad things really are, that won't help.

Provide distractions

There is something that the victim needs as often as possible and that is to be distracted from the situation at home. The more time that they can be distracted, the more chance they have of seeing that there is a better life for them.

This also gives you more opportunity to talk to them about their situation and hopefully steer them away from the abuse.

The thing with doing this and one of the problems with it is that the abuser will not necessarily like it. You have to be careful that you balance this as you do not want to cause them more problems at home. More often than not the victim will not tell you that it is in fact causing them more problems, so you need to be sensitive to them and make sure that you keep thing in balance.

Provide Information

What I am talking about here is not just providing them information that deals with domestic abuse and the situation, but also providing them information that will help them to grow as a person to the point where they can do something about the situation.

The sort of information you need to provide them with should be information on building their self-esteem and dignity. There is a lot of information and books available on this topic and a lot of it will provide them with tips and advice that can help to get them moving in the right direction.

Once again, subtlety is the key in doing this. Share the information with them, don't force it on them.

Smile and Nod

Here is one for the victim to use, and that is to smile and nod. Generally speaking the abuse comes with a lot of anger, and therefore one of the things that they do want to be doing is not giving the abuser cause to be angry.

The idea behind smile and nod is to basically make sure that the abuser gets what they want, at least on the surface. The key to this is that the victim is doing it intentionally to make them think that they are getting what they want, and that they are in control, but the victim is the one that is in control because they are smiling and nodding so as to avoid a situation that they do not want.

Control is very much a mental thing, and if the victim is doing this consciously, then they are not being controlled.

This is something that you can encourage the victim to do when they have started to gain some self-respect and dignity back and they are now starting to regain control and moving to the point where they can break free of the abuse. In the mean time they want to make sure that they minimise the abuse. Sometimes it is not a matter of standing up to the abuser, sometimes it is just a matter of keeping the peace until the time comes to break free of the abuse and the relationship.

Where can they get help?

I am sure the list of organisations that provide help for victims and abusers in domestic abuse could fill a whole telephone directory, but that is not what this chapter is about.

The fact is that this problem is so rife in society that there are a vast number of places where help is available. I think the best place to start would be with the GP or family doctor. They will know the best people in the local area to talk to, and they are usually people that the victim can trust to talk about what is going on.

The other place is the police. I am not suggesting that the victim go to the police to get action taken against the abuser, but they will also know the places in the local area where a victim can get support.

Ange and I are available to offer support and we can be contacted through the website (www.smellthereality.com).

Another good website that I recommend is www.hiddenhurt.co.uk. They have an anonymous forum on there where you and or the victim can communicate with others in a similar situation.

Reading books like this one are also designed to help. You can never have too much information. The more they understand the situation they are in, the better equipped they will be to deal with it. It is not just the current situation that they need to deal with; they also need to be thinking about what they are going to do after the move. In the next section I am going to give some information on that, but like I said you can never have too much information.

It is important that the victim knows that they are not alone, and there is a huge amount of support and help available to them, but they have to be ready to go and get it and then accept the help once they have found it.

END OF THE SECTION

Throughout this section I have talked about some of the things that you can do as a friend or loved one of a victim of domestic abuse. This section has not provided hard and fast rules, this is deliberate.

Throughout this book I have focussed on providing information, insight and guidance and not rigid rules. Once again it is the ideas that are important and how you can apply the information that I have provided you with to make things better in your world.

What I have done is hopefully given you enough to think about and outlined enough of the pitfalls and problems that are associated with trying to help a victim in order to make your job a bit easier.

Every person and every situation is different, and the way that you approach them to offer your help will also be different. That is for you to decide, and for you to think about the most effective way to help the victim. Always keep in mind that this is what it is all about, helping the victim to grow to be able to do something about the situation. Sneaking in, in the middle of the night and forcibly removing them from the situation may look good in the movies, but in the real world it is not going to help.

You need to be patient and gentle, sensitive to the needs of the victim and have a good understanding of the abusive situation and ways to help as I have provided you throughout this book. When you bring it all together, you should be able to make a real difference to someone's life.

To The Victim

*I*n this section I am going to address everything to the victim. It does not mean that everyone should not read it. If you are helping a victim, then the information that is in this section will also give you ideas about some of the things that you can discuss with the people you are trying to help.

If you are an abuser, the information here will help you realise what it is you are actually doing to the victim. If all of the information you have read so far has not helped you to understand this fully, then this section will help to drive the point home.

To the victim, the first thing that I want to say is that I apologize for referring to you all the time as a victim. I understand that you are a person and are much more than just a victim, however for the purpose of this book it was necessary to make sure that I did not get caught in any stereotypes and so I had to use something that was understandable and recognisable throughout.

In this section I am going to talk directly referring to you as a person. Firstly I am going to be talking about some of the things that you need to keep in mind that will help you to gain some self-respect and dignity. Then we are going to talk about how you can keep working on yourself to get to the point where you are ready to do something about your situation, and then we are going to talk about what happens to you after you break free.

This is a book about domestic abuse, but it is also about people. The domestic abuse is the theme, but it is the people that it is aimed at. A lot of emphasis is put on dealing with the situation, but very often the person gets almost ignored after the situation is dealt with.

I think it is important to look at the person that is left at the end of the abuse, and think about the life that they will have to rebuild. The abuse is something that happens to someone, it does not have to define them as a person for the rest of their lives.

Once again I will point out that the information here is general, and is not aimed at your specific situation. You have to use your judgment and understanding of the exact nature of your situation and use the information throughout this book as you see fit and as it applies to your situation.

I do not know you, I do not know your situation and I do not know the abuser. I do not know what they are capable of and I do not know the extent that you have suffered. I do know people in general and I do know that the information in this book is accurate as a general overview of this subject.

Please take what you can from here, think about it and how it relates to you and your situation.

LIFE IN A BLACK HOLE

I bet you know what I am talking about when I say living with domestic abuse is like living in a black hole. You are trapped and there is nothing that you can do to get out. There is no light at the end of the tunnel and sometimes you are not even sure which way is up. You spend your life in various shades of darkness and you don't even dare to dream of what it would be like to get out of the hole.

Some days you feel like you are hanging on to the sides by your finger nails, and other days you feel like you are in freefall. There are even some days where you think that you are actually clawing your way to the top and then all of a sudden someone stands on you and you fall back down again.

The reason that I put in this chapter is because I want you to know that you are not alone, which may be a good thing to know and all that but it is not going to help your situation. That is true, but it is also important that you understand that I do understand something about where you are and that I am going to try and help you change things. I guess that I am asking you to trust me a little here.

You need to trust me when I tell you that there is light at the end of the tunnel, you may not be able to see it just yet, but it is there. I can't tell you how long the tunnel is or how many things you are going to trip over on your way there, but I will tell you that there is a way out, and there is hope.

I mentioned earlier that as long as we continue to draw breath, there is hope. This section is all about helping to change some things about yourself that will start you moving to the end of the tunnel, and help you to dig your way out of the hole.

It can be done, it has been done many times before, and it can be done by you. You may not feel it, but you are a lot stronger than you realise and there are many more things about yourself that I am going to help you to discover, or rediscover, whichever the case may be.

Hang in there, don't give up hope and keep reading. You may just find that little spark that you are looking for that will help you get your fire going again.

YOU ARE MORE THAN A VICTIM

Throughout our lives, we, as people tend to get defined by the things that happen to us and the labels that get put on us. Once that happens we find ourselves living in a certain way so as to justify the labels that have been put on us or live up to these labels. What then happens is that we sometimes lose our individuality or identity. We must always remember that first and foremost we are unique individuals and not what we are labelled by the society.

I am going to use myself as an example here to give you an idea of what I am talking about. Now I have many categories that I fall into, and therefore I am defined by those roles depending on the situation that I am in and who I am dealing with.

Right now, as I am sitting writing this I am an author. Now that label itself comes with an image that is instantly placed on me. Straight away you will form some kind of image of me based on that information.

However at the same time I am also a parent, a step-father, a husband, a brother, a son, a son-in-law, and many other things. Each of these things comes with its own set of rules and expectations that are built into it. I have also been many other things that I am no longer. For example I worked in computers for many years, throughout that time I was a programmer, a support person, a manager, a team member, a software designer and a number of other things as well. Now you may think that these are just job titles, and they are, but at the same time they are labels that come to define how I am supposed to act, the things I am supposed to know and how people will treat me.

But the thing that I always try and keep in mind is that before any of those things I am just me. I am Brian and as Brian there are things that I like and things that I don't. There are times when I am happy and sad, there are times when I am energetic and there are times when I am tired etc. You see when you get back to the basics, it becomes different again. When people understand the label and group that I fit into, they know roughly what to expect from me, and therefore how they should treat me, plus all of the stereotypes that come to be associated with that particular group.

But at the same time, I also define myself according to the labels and groups, and therefore the expectations that I put on myself accordingly also change. For example, as an author it is my job to write. There are times when I do not want to write, however as an author I should be writing. What this means is that I put pressure on myself to produce.

It is very easy to lose who you are in the whole mix of labels and expectations that are put on you. Sometimes it is OK just to be you. Sometimes it is not OK to have to live up to the label that is put on you, even if you created the label.

What this is all leading to is that because you have labelled yourself a victim, or someone else has labelled you a victim, it does not mean that it is that label that must define you as a person. Being a victim is something that has happened to you, it does not define you as a person. The same as being a partner or spouse does not define you. A relationship; married or otherwise, is a joining of two people to form a third entity – the relationship. It does not mean that the two people do not exist anymore. It just means that they are now a part of something else, as well.

Being a victim of domestic abuse is also something that you are, but it does not mean that the person no longer exists. Being a victim is a situation and a label, not a description of a person.

In the same way being a parent is a role that an individual takes on, it does not mean that they need to surrender who they are, it simply means that they have children and they have the responsibilities, pressures, joys etc that come with that role.

The point to all of this is that you do not have to lose the person that you are just because of the labels and roles that you take on as you go through life. People tend to forget that we are individuals and we come to be defined by the group or category that we fit into.

Before you were in this relationship, before you were abused and before you became a victim, you were a person; an individual. That does not change, and it is that person and that individual that you need to recognise again.

It is that person with all the strengths and weaknesses, all of the good points and all of the bad points that you need to recapture and think about who that person was and what they wanted from life. What they set out to achieve, and also what has been taken from them throughout the journey of life.

You are a person and individual, before you are a part of any group or category. Don't let the things that you do, and the roles that you perform define who you are.

Being YOU is all the definition that you need.

DON'T THINK LIKE A VICTIM

One of the things that I think is important to say at this point is that you must not think like a victim. I know that throughout this book I have spoken about how it is not until you realise that you are a victim of domestic abuse that you can do something about it, and now I am telling you something different, in fact I am telling you the complete opposite.

There is a reason for this, and if you look at the previous chapter it should start to make a little more sense why I am now saying that you need to stop thinking like a victim.

The thing with victims is that stuff always happens to them. I mentioned this earlier in the book, about how some people just seem to give out the wrong kind of vibes, and therefore they get treated accordingly, well this is similar, but not quite the same thing.

When you think of yourself as a victim then it gives you an opportunity to justify all of the bad things that have happened to you and therefore it means that you do not have to accept responsibility for it. I am sure you know what I am talking about. I guess you know someone who is the unluckiest person in the world. No matter what happens they always seem to just have bad stuff happen to them all the time, they are always the victim of something or other.

Now if you think about it, they never do anything wrong, it just seems that the whole world is against them. I could even be talking about you, I don't know, but you will get what I am talking about either way. These are also generally the same people that think that everyone else is lucky.

They are the ones that see someone else who has money, nice cars, nice houses, good kids, good social life and all that, and they point to them and wish they were as 'lucky' as them. But the only luck they seem to get is all bad.

What these people are, are victims. They are victims of life. You see they are the ones that plan their future by counting on winning the lottery or somehow getting lucky. Instead of looking at where they are located in life and accepting that they are where they are because they made the choices that they did. The same way the 'lucky' people who have the nice things made their choices to get the things that they have.

I know that you did not choose to be a victim of domestic abuse, nobody ever does, but at the end of the day you have made choices along the way that have put you in the position that you are now. Don't think for a second that I am getting into the blame game here or saying that you chose to be like this, I am not.

What I am saying is that the choices that you have made along the way have led you to where you are. Well not the choices that you made so much as the consequences of the choices that you made. Although the consequences were not known at the time of making the choice that you made, they are a result of the choices that you made.

Let me put that into context so that you can understand this point clearly, you chose the partner that you now have. At some point you decided that you wanted to be with them and wanted to have a relationship with them. Now at the time you did not know that they were going to turn out to be abusive, but nonetheless, you did choose to be with them.

What happened since then is that the relationship changed, and the person that you thought you were getting involved with changed. They made you into the victim, and they took on the role of the abuser. That is pretty much a fact, given that I believe that I am talking to the victim of domestic abuse.

So now you think of yourself as a victim, and therefore it makes you think that as a victim you do not have any control or say in the matter. And to a certain extent you may be correct. Given that an abuser is the one that assumes the control over everything.

Now we start getting to the main point here. Whilst you think of yourself as a victim, you will be a victim. Because a victim has no control, you defer that control to the abuser.

There is one thing that the abuser does not have control over, if you do not allow them to have control over it, and that is the way that you think and the way that you feel. They like you to think and feel a certain way, and guide you, and lead you to that point, but here is the thing, they are only able to actually do that, because you allow them to.

Being a victim allows you to do this, because it is not your fault, and you just do what you have to do to get through the day. Keep in mind that this is exactly what the abuser wants you to think. They want you to feel like a victim and therefore you pass all the control to them, and then they essentially own you. Now I am not saying that you do this on purpose, and I am not saying that it is even something that you knew was happening, and if we are honest the abuser probably does not even know all of this either.

What I wanted to tell you all this for is because once you are aware of this kind of thing, then you can do something about it. There is no reason to think that you should be able to do something that you know nothing about. If I were to give all the parts that make up a car, and say build me a car, you are probably not going to be able to do it; because firstly you do not know how to build a car and secondly you do not have the tools to build a car.

What I given you so far in this chapter is the knowledge and understanding of what has happened, now I am going to give you some of the tools that you can use to fix the problem.

The starting point is to stop thinking of yourself as A victim. In this situation you are THE victim of the situation and you are THE victim of the abuser, but as a person you are not a victim, you are a person. This may look like I am playing word games, but this is really very important. How you view yourself is one of the things that is keeping you where you are. You need to change the way that you see yourself and the way that you think about yourself before you can even start to change the situation.

Now that you are not a victim anymore, but you are the victim, you now have the control over the way that you think and feel and you also have the power back over you, as a person. OK you still do not have the power over your situation, sadly the abuser still has that, but you have to start somewhere, and that somewhere is with you as a person.

What I mean when I talk about how you do not have to allow the abuser to control how you think and how you feel is that those things are yours to do with as you wish. The abuser wants you to think about yourself in a certain way and they want you to think about them in a certain way, and for the most part you probably go along with this. But you do not have to. The abuser does not need to know how you are thinking and how you are feeling; they only need to know that they believe they are getting what they wanted. If you read the previous section you will remember that I talked about Smile and Nod, and this is where that comes into play.

As far as the abuser is concerned, they are in control because you are not fighting back and you are doing everything that they want, so they do not need to worry about anything. On the inside however you are doing it for a completely different reason, you are doing it because you just need to get through without causing hassle. So instead of the abuser being in control, you are actually in control because now you are manipulating the situation instead of it manipulating you.

I am not saying that is easy to do, because it is not. I am not saying that this is going to solve your self-esteem problems, because it is not. I am not saying that it is going to make you like yourself more, because it is not. What I am saying is that the first thing you need to do is to take back control over yourself.

The abuser has been manipulating you to think and feel a certain way, through various methods, but you will find that for the most part they have done what they wanted because you have allowed them to make you think and feel the way that they wanted you to.

Now that you know about this and how it works, the good part is that you can change it. You can take back that control, and you can start to be that person that was there before they became a victim.

Just because you are doing this, there is no reason why you need to change the way things are at home, because that is not easy, and I do not want to cause you more pain because all of a sudden you feel you can stand up to the abuser, because that is not the case. Take this on board, start to think like a person and not a victim, it is the first step to regaining you.

There is a down side to this however, and that is now that the abuse becomes a little worse because you now see it as pure abuse, and you now start to realise just how badly you have been treated. It is almost like the abuse becomes personal again. This will lead to lots of ups and downs. It will mean that when the abuse comes, it will drag you down a little more, but the other side is that once it does drag you down, hang on to the fact that you will find a way out of this.

As a person you do not have to be subjected to this, you are the one that is in control of your thoughts and your emotions. They may have control physically, they may have control of the environment, but they do not control the real you. You have just found that person again, and you are not going to surrender it again, to anyone.

Please keep this in mind as much as you can. It is easy for me to write it here, but it is not as easy as it sounds. It is going to take a lot of work to change the way that you think.

Essentially you have to change your automatic thinking processes. Your natural thinking has been changed over time to become the way that you are now, and it will take a period of time to change it to the way that I am suggesting. About the best advice I give you on this, is to try and look at the way that you think. Most people never do it. Most people never understand that they are in control of the way that they think, and they never bother to think about thinking.

What I am asking you to do is exactly that. Think about how you are thinking. I want you to catch yourself thinking like a victim and I want you to replace that thought with the things that we have talked about here. It will take time, it does not just happen because you have read it in a book, but it can be done.

It can be done without the abuser knowing about it, and therefore it is not something that you need to seek permission from them to do. It is something that is personal to you and something that you can do at any time, without disrupting anything else.

Think about the way you think, stop thinking like a victim, change that victim mentality and you are on the path to becoming a winner.

You do deserve to have better

One of the things that an abuser will constantly tell you is that you are getting all that you deserve, and sooner or later you come to believe it. This is what happens as your self-respect and dignity are eroded away. The abuser will tell you this because they do not want you thinking that you are better than what they are trying to make you and they do not want you thinking that there is more out there for you than there is at home.

You see now how it is that they control the way that you are thinking; by making you think and believe the things that they want you to believe. This is where it is important for you to recapture your own thoughts and beliefs and start thinking as a person and not a victim.

I am going to tell you something that I am sure others have told you and as much as you want to believe, you are almost too afraid to because all it does is get your hopes up and then it makes it harder to face up to the reality of your situation. I understand that it can be like that, but you also have to realise that if you do not have hope, then you are left with despair. When you are clouded in despair then you are not going to be able to do anything about the situation.

The thing with hope is that it is the same as your thoughts and your feelings, it is something that is personal to you and it is something that the abuser cannot do anything about, if you don't let them.

Now that you are aware that you can control these things, I want you to think about your life and I want you to think about how you wanted it to be and how it has turned out. I am sure you will find there is a very big gap in there somewhere, but the good thing is that it does not always have to be this way.

I am not going to tell you that you should go and pack all of your things and leave, it is not that simple, but I want you to know that it does not have to be like this forever and that you do deserve more than life has given you so far.

Here is something for you to think about; would you wish your life and your relationship on another person? Even if you did not like them; I am sure that you would be thinking that you would not. Now ask yourself, why not?

I am going to go out on a bit of limb and suggest that it is because they do not deserve it. Even if you do not like them, you do not think they deserve to be stuck in the situation that you find yourself in.

So the next question then has to be, if they do not deserve it, what makes you think that you do?

Earlier in the book I spoke about your rights, but what I am talking about here goes beyond that. What I am talking about here is that as a person there is no reason for you to think that you deserve to live in a place where you are mistreated and abused by your partner.

Not only do you not deserve to be dominated and controlled, your partner does not deserve to have that control and power over you. If you are honest, there are lots of things that they deserve, but control over you as a person is most certainly not one of them.

Everybody deserves to be able to think and feel what they want to. Every person deserves to be happy in their life and be able to do the things that they want to do. Provided that it does not to infringe on other people and their rights, every person deserves to be free. Thousands of people have fought wars and died so that you are able to live free and be free. They deserve to be respected for what they did and you show that respect for them by living with the understanding that you deserve to live a life of freedom. You deserve a life free of fear and persecution and free from victimisation. Everybody deserves this.

There is something else that everyone deserves and that is a chance to be happy. Being happy is one of those things that means different things to different people, but every one of us deserves to be happy doing the things that we want to do that makes us happy.

Regardless of what anyone tells you, these are the things that every person deserves. You are no different, and the things that you want are not that different to thousands of other people; they are not more deserving than you.

The reason this chapter is so important is because it is directly related to your self-esteem. It is your sense of you and how you feel about you that is going to have a huge impact on your life. As I mentioned earlier it is the sense of self-respect and pride that is ultimately going to empower you enough to do something about your situation.

If you do not feel that you as a person are worthy of anymore than you have, then you are not going to be trying to reach for it. It is a huge barrier that is in the way.

This is not just true of you and your situation; this is true of all people everywhere. The reason that some people really succeed and get everything they want in life, and a lot more others do not is because some people believe that that they are worthy and therefore deserve the things that they want. Once they have decided that they deserve it, they then do the things that they need to do to make sure they get what they deserve. A lot of other people believe that what they have is what they deserve, so they do not reach for anything else. It is what is called a glass ceiling. When we feel we have reached our glass ceiling, we stop trying. That is what happens to people in domestic abuse situations; when they stop believing that they deserve anything else; they stop reaching and trying to find a way out.

Let me give you an example that will help to make it clearer. Have you ever seen an elephant at the circus or on TV and noticed how they are only restrained by a small piece of string around their ankle tied to a small peg in the ground. Have you ever wondered why the elephant does not simply pull on the string and either snap it or pull the peg out of the ground? It is not because they are trained to stand still, if that were the case then they would not need to be tied up. The reason is because when they were first tied around the ankle it was with a chain and the other end was tied to something that even an elephant could not break. During this time the elephant would pull and pull until it came to know that it simply could not break away. Once the elephant comes to know that they are not going to be able to get away, they simply stop pulling. It is then that they are able to be restrained by a small piece of string on a peg in the ground, because they do not pull against it.

The same thing applies to people who believe that they have got what they deserve, they stop pulling, even if it is just a small piece of string around a peg, they never pull against it, so they never know that there is a world waiting out there, but they need to break free to get at it.

You do deserve to have the sort of life that you always wanted, regardless of what anyone will tell you. You do deserve the sort of life that you always wanted, regardless of what you tell yourself and what you have come to believe.

I am not telling you that it is going to be easy and I am not telling you that it can happen overnight, all I am telling you is that you need to realise that nobody deserves to be treated like you are being treated, and no matter what anyone will tell you, you are a worthy and deserving person and you deserve to be happy and free.

The best thing that you can do is to try and remind yourself of this as often as possible. I do not know your situation, but if you can keep this book handy and re-read these things when it is all looking bleak and terrible it will help you to remind yourself of all of the things that we have talked about. Alternatively find something that you can use that will remind you of the life that you always wanted so that you can tell yourself that you do deserve a better life.

THINK ABOUT WHAT YOU OWE

What I am talking about here is not what you owe in financial terms but what you owe others as a person.

In dealing with abuse situations one of the things that I have encountered is that the victim comes to believe that they owe huge debts to all of the people around them, and that is one of the reasons that they are stuck in the relationship.

This is another one of those things that the abuser will want the victim to believe. They will be telling you that you have ruined their life and you owe it to them to make amends for it. They will tell you that you have ruined the kids' lives and you owe it to them to make amends for it.

I am sure there are also other people around you that like to make you think that you owe them something also.

Here is the thing with these kinds of so called debts; they do not really exist in the terms that I mentioned above. What they are, are barriers. They are barriers that are put in place by other people to control what you think and how you behave.

There is one person on this planet that you owe something to, and that is yourself. All the other debts are created by other people. You do not owe other people any more than what you feel you owe them. When it comes to debts like this you have to go with what you honestly feel about it. Ultimately it is for you to decide whether you owe people anything or not. It is about how comfortable you feel about yourself, and whether or not you honestly believe that there are moral debts and obligations out there for you. These debts and obligations need to be set by you and for you; they are not for someone else to place upon you, because they feel you owe them something. It doesn't work that way.

Let's have a look at what you actually owe the abuser. I am sure that at some point you will have made promises to them, whether that was in a marriage vow or not, at some stage you will have committed yourself to them. Chances are at some point they also did the same to you. Now if you think about it, have they honoured their commitment to you, have they even gone above and beyond that commitment to the point where you actually owe them something in return?

Generally speaking the answer to that is NO. As adults you both are in the relationship; and any relationship involves a degree of risk. You and your partner must understand that a relationship involves a degree of risk and therefore it does not come with any guarantees, and therefore there are no refunds or debts that can accumulate from it.

When it comes to children it is a little different, because as a parent you do owe it your children to make sure they are getting the best that you can give them. It does not mean that you have to sacrifice your life for them, and it does not mean you have to sell your soul for them. What it means is that you do the best that you can to help them grow into good and decent people. Having said that, you have to ask yourself if the environment that you are in is the best place to raise them to be good and decent people? Maybe there is a debt that you should think about. You do owe your children the best that you can give them. That is not the best that you can give them financially, it is the best you can give them as people. Think about that one a little more.

Do not think that you owe your partner some kind of moral debt, because it is simply not true. You do not owe them anything. You do owe it to yourself to do all that you can to become the kind of person that you want to become. You do owe it to your children to provide them the best environment for them to learn and grow to become good and decent people.

Do not always believe that you owe anyone anything without examining the situation and deciding for yourself if you owe them a debt or not. A moral obligation is something that comes from within and something that you place on yourself, it is not something someone can send you a bill for and simply demand that you pay it. That is not the way that it works.

The reason that I am talking about things like this is because I want you to see that these things are all barriers that are put in your way to keep you where you are. They are created by others, and it is done in such a way as to make you believe them.

I did mention earlier that if you throw a decent amount of reality at a barrier then it will not often hold up under the pressure. Start seeing the barriers for what they are, and try to reason your way through them and around them.

Now you see why it was important to change the way that you are thinking, because now that you are thinking differently you can start to see things in a different light. You start to see things as they really are, and you start to realise that a lot of the things you have been told and have come to believe are really not true.

You start to believe in yourself as a person and an individual who has more to offer in life than being a victim and a slave to an abuser. Keep going forward, keep thinking, keep growing and ultimately you will get to the point where you can break free and be the best that you can be.

IT IS NOT YOUR FAULT

This may or may not be the first time that someone has told you this. Maybe you have never told anyone that you think it is your fault before and so nobody has ever told you that it is not your fault. If someone has told you this before, then it is most likely that you did not believe them anyway.

I am going to tell you this again and I am also going to tell you why it is not your fault. It might appear that I am laying the blame on someone else but I have to say that it is the abusers fault. I do not want to judge them harshly because I understand that there are lots of situations and circumstances that happen along the way that make them that way. I am not absolving them from their responsibility, but I am not blaming them either, but ultimately it is the abuser that is treating you that way, and to be honest I do not think there is anything that can honestly justify that. So having said that, I want to get back to the main focus here and that is explaining to you why it is not your fault.

We are going right back to the beginning of your relationship and we will look at how things started out and then progressed to the point that they are at the moment. Along the way I want you to think about the point at which things changed, and what you actually did to make things change to the degree that they have.

In the beginning you met your partner and you went through a courtship period. Over time you would be spending more and more time together. It would have gotten to the point where you were probably only apart because it was unavoidable.

During this time there would have been talk about some kind of future together. Whilst this talk of the future was going on there would have been no hint of abuse or a suggestion that your life would be a misery.

Looking back now there may have been signs that they were dominant and controlling, and perhaps you even thought that over time you could change them. Even if this was the case, it does not mean that you have to suffer for the rest of your life because you made an error in judgment.

It may not have even been like that at all, it could be that it did not start until much later. When you were living together and life wasn't really working out like it was all planned when you were spending all that time together and planning the dream future.

It could be that somewhere along the way you stopped liking each other, got bored, no money, no work, kids, debts and all the other things that we call life. It could be that as these things happened then the nastiness started coming out, slowly at first, but got progressively worse. You probably went through some of the things that I mentioned earlier, the talking through things, the promises to change, the once last chance.

I could be completely off the mark here, as I said I don't know you, but this scenario is not that uncommon. The point is not to test how psychic I am, the point is that I wanted you to look back at your relationship and start picking out some of the key moments along the way that you can identify as being some the early stages of the abuse.

I want you to think about how it came about, and then I want you think about what you did wrong throughout that time that caused both of you to fall out with each other to the point that things got so terribly bad that the abuser had to start treating you the way that they do.

I want you to think about the time that you have been together and how you are personally responsible for what has gone on in the past, the things that you did to make it so that the abuser felt that rather than leave the relationship, they owed it to the world to make sure you would not do the same thing to someone else.

Let us not forget that throughout all of this, if the abuser was that desperately unhappy with you and with the relationship at any time that they could have left and started again. There was nothing keeping them there in order to abuse you.

Maybe things did not work out as you had planned; but if you can show me any couple who's relationship has worked out as perfect as they had planned it in the beginning I would dearly love to meet them.

Here is something to think about when it comes to people and how they imagine things. There are two ways that people think about the outcome of things. Firstly there is the way that they hope it will turn out. What this is; is the ideal version of everything, with nothing negative; it is all good all the time. The relationship is perfect, there are never any arguments. The house is big and pretty. There are big gardens, nice cars. A dog and kids running in the yard, it is always a nice sunny day. The grass is always cut and everything is just 'nice'. This is how we imagine the things that we want, the best possible way that we can think of.

On the other hand there are the times when we imagine the things that we don't want. This is generally when we have to do something or are confronted with something that there is no way out off, and so when we imagine this, we imagine the worst case scenario. This is what fear does to us, it makes us think the worse possible thing that we can about the thing that we are afraid of. Generally it is not anywhere near as bad as we thought it would be, but nonetheless that is how we think about it.

What you get in the real world is something that is in between those two extremes. The future can be happy, but rarely is going to be anything like you imagine it to be; on the other hand the things that you don't like are rarely as bad as you thought they were going to be; it is called Reality.

So if you keep that in mind, and also keep in mind that really nobody believes that all of the dreams are all going to come true, then please think about at what point did you fail so badly in your side of the arrangement and your side of the relationship that meant that it was your fault by way of the things that you did that led to the abuse.

From there I want you to think about all of the things that you keep doing, each and every day, that suggests it is your fault that the abuse continues. How did you, and do you continue to fail so badly to justify being treated like you are?

When I look at these relationship the only thing a victim can be accused of doing wrong is trying to believe the best of their partner and trying to see past the bad points to keep the relationship alive and taking no action against the abuser until the abusive situation gets out of hand and they are held captive.

In my opinion that is not something that you can blame anyone for. Trusting and loving are honourable traits, not something to be punished for. If anything you can blame yourself for being too soft and for trying to live your dream and not doing something earlier, but I do not think you can blame anyone for caring too much.

Sadly there are people that will take advantage of this side of people. There are people that will take advantage of the loving and gentler side of another person and exploit and use them for their own gains. Maybe you have to consider that your partner is one of these people.

Loving and caring is not a fault, it can be exploited, but it is never a fault.

So what else do you think you did that stopped the partner from walking away from the relationship when they obviously were not happy with it and it was not working out for them?

At what point did you and your partner agree that you would rather be abused and degraded continually for years to come, rather than them leaving the relationship?

I know that along the way there could have been children and mortgages and all sorts of other commitments, but none of these things can justify your partner abusing you rather than moving on with their life; if they are unhappy with you as a partner.

The idea behind this chapter is to make you think about your relationship and how it has gotten to this point. It is to make you think about the things that you did that were so terribly wrong that it is your fault that your partner is treating you this way.

OK, you could go down the path of fact that it is your fault because you did stay, and you continue to stay, I think we have more than squashed that whole argument throughout this book.

Once again, the fact that you think it is your fault is nothing more than another barrier and excuse put there by the abuser to stop you leaving and to justify what they are doing. It is nothing more than that, and you are certainly not to blame for the actions of someone else.

Here is something else for you to think about whilst we are on this subject. Throughout this book I have mentioned how we are all responsible for the choices that we make. This most certainly applies to the abuser. Keep in mind that they have also chosen to stay in this relationship and they have chosen to continue with the abuse. Even if there were reasons why it just sort of crept in unnoticed, at some point they must have come to the conclusion that they do not love and respect you anymore or they simply would not be able to do this to you. They are choosing this, not you, they have the power and the control, not you, and they could stop it, whereas you have not been able to.

Please think very carefully about these things, and I am sure that there is no way that you could argue that it is your fault that you are treated in this way, at least not if you are honest with yourself.

I HOPE I AM NOT SCARING YOU

As I am writing this I realised that a lot of the stuff that we have talked about, whilst it makes sense and it will help you, can also seem a bit daunting.

If you think about it, I have asked you to do nothing more than think about things. I have not asked you to do anything other than change the way that you are thinking and I have tried to help you to remove some of the barriers that have been put in the way by you or by someone else.

But this in itself can also be very frightening and I do understand that. Once you start changing the way that you think and you start seeing things the way they really are it sort of shatters all of the things that you have been hanging onto in order to survive the way that you do.

It makes a myth out of all of the things that you have been telling yourself in order to make it better and acceptable and perhaps the biggest thing that it does is remove your comfort zone. Even though you are not happy with the way things are and you are not happy with the way you are being treated it has become familiar to you and therefore it has become your comfort zone.

Of all of the things that I have been talking about the fact that your world is being stripped bare and your comfort zone is being torn down can be far scarier than the abuse that you have to deal with.

It is not my intention to scare you and it is not my intention to make a mockery of everything you have come to believe in. I am simply trying to help you see things as they really are. Once you accept the reality of your situation and see people for who they really are, then you can work out what you are going to do about it.

If you are reading this book it is because you want to understand more and because you want to change your life. To break out of an abusive relationship is perhaps one of the hardest things you will ever have to do, but it is also one of the most rewarding and beneficial things you will ever do.

I do not think that I need to tell you how the benefits outweigh the pain in this instance. I think you already know that and I think that you have already figured out that this is not the way you want to live anymore, otherwise you would not be reading this book.

None of the things that I have asked you to do are going to happen overnight. All of the things are going to happen slowly if you understand them, think about them and work at them.

Not one of them involves anything more than looking at the way you are thinking, changing the way you are thinking and dispelling some of the more common myths that exist in this situation. I have not and will not suggest anything other than things that will help you as a person get a better handle on yourself and the things around you.

I am not suggesting that you need to leave your family and kids, I am not suggesting that you need to put yourself at risk, I am not suggesting that you need to put yourself in danger by standing up to the abuser, it would be irresponsible for me to do that given that I know nothing about you and your situation.

All I am asking you do, and all I am suggesting is just to look at things honestly, break down the barriers that are in place around you so you can get a clear view. It is only then that YOU can decide what you can and will do about it.

What I am trying to do is to make you start to feel good about yourself because you have reason to feel good about yourself. I am trying to do that by shattering some of the illusions and giving you some reality. All of the things that I am telling you here are true in general, and will apply to you and your situation in some way.

I am not telling you that you are anything that you are not, and

I am not painting a nice rosy picture that is going to come crashing down around you as soon as you close the book.

Don't be scared to think for yourself and don't be afraid to live in reality; that is the place that you need to make the changes if you want things to change.

If you keep doing what you are doing; you will keep getting what you are getting. Think about that.

CONTROL IS IN THE MIND

We have touched on this throughout the book but I wanted to go over it again in more detail because it is a very important thing to understand. If you go back a couple of chapters where I spoke about Smile and Nod, that is essentially the kind of thing that I am talking about when I say that control is in the mind.

To a certain degree the abuser has the control over you because they have control over the way that you think. We have spoken about how you can get that control back from them, but it is a critical piece of the puzzle so I am going to talk about it a little more.

When an abusive relationship is not physical, then the control is 100% in the mind. If there is violence then obviously there is a degree of physical control in place, but there is also a large degree of control that is going on in the mind also. Part of that control comes from the fear of the physical abuse, but there is also a great deal more to it than that.

Throughout this book I have talked about how control and power are the things that the abuser is looking for, and I have spoken about control in a number of different ways, and I think that it is perhaps the most essential thing that you need to understand if you are going to be able to do something about it.

Control is something people seek throughout their entire lives in one form or another, it is fair to say that this is perhaps more of a male trait than a female trait, but ultimately it is something that exists in all of us in one form or another and to differing degrees also.

I know for myself I am a bit of a control freak; however the thing that I like to be in control of is me. I am very dedicated and very disciplined when it comes to being in control of myself. At times this control does spill over to the world around me, and therefore to the people around me, but for the most part I like to be in control of me. For that reason I do not drink; or at least I drink so rarely that it is pretty much a non-starter. I don't drink, because I want to be in control of me and my mind.

The thing with an abuser is that they feel the need to control other people, and focus less perhaps on controlling themselves. Their need to control someone else, namely you, is one of the things that keeps them doing what they are doing. There are a lot of other things that are going on as well, but control is certainly a big part of it. The thing with control is that most of it occurs in the mind. Firstly it is in their mind where they believe they are controlling you, and secondly it gets into your mind when you buy into the belief that they are controlling you. It could even get to the point where you are unable to think for yourself because the abuser does all of the thinking for you.

Once you buy into the fact that they have control, it becomes a bit like the elephant that I spoke of earlier; you just allow them that control and don't question it. Again, this is not something that you decide to do, it just sort of happens.

What you need to understand here is that the abuser has no way of knowing what you are thinking unless you tell them or do something that shows what you are thinking. This is what makes the 'smile and nod' thing work. Although you are acting in a way that is agreeable to them, you are in control of you. It may seem like this is inconsequential when you think about it, but on the other hand it is perhaps the key starting to regain control in your life.

It is a bit like going to the dentist. If you have to go to the dentist because you have a toothache and need a filling or a tooth taken out, you will absolutely hate it from the moment that you make the appointment to the time that you have to go.

On the other hand if you were going to get a set of nice new veneers put on your teeth, then you will be excited about the trip to the dentist. In fact it would probably be fair to say that the time could not come quickly enough. The point is that the dentist is still going to be doing the same thing, i.e. poking about in your mouth and all the other things that they do, but because the reason is different it seems to make all of the difference in the world. The only thing that is really different is the way that you approach it, which comes down to the way that you think about it.

Basically in the second scenario you are doing it because you want to, and in the first you are doing it because you have to. In the second you are in control, at least in your mind you are in control.

So you see how you can make a real difference to a situation simply by changing the way that you think about it. It is a case of who is in control, it is crucial for you be in control of yourself because it is when you are in control of yourself that you can then start firstly to be yourself, and secondly start thinking about the things you want to think of without fear.

It does not mean that you will behave any differently, remember that you have to be thinking about the things that you want. The first thing that you want is not to be abused, so the last thing that you want to do is something that is going to upset the abuser and cause them to kick off. It may be that in the past that you may do something just to wind them up, not because you want to bring the abuse, but because you want to get at them, but when you come to think about it, it is never a clever thing to do.

If you really want to get back at them then start thinking about all of the things that you have been reading about in this book. Reclaim you as a person, reclaim the control over your own thoughts and emotions, and stop the control that they have. The beauty of this is that they do not even know about it, and yet everything they have been working towards has slipped away from them and they do not even know it.

Remember that control exists in two places; the abusers mind and the victim's mind; that is when it is absolute. When you take back that control from them, then the power is instantly more than halved because you are now in control of yourself, and you can then start to control the situations a little so that they still think they are pacified, but they are pacified because YOU want them to be, not because they have won and are in control.

If you think about it, when a baby is screaming and going off, then you give them a dummy to pacify them so that you can have some peace, and really this is no different. You want the abuser pacified, so you can have some peace, that is you manipulating the situation and that is you manipulating them, simply by changing the way that you think about things.

It is a small thing on the surface, but it has huge implications and can have a huge impact on you and the rest of your life. Please think very carefully about this and you will see how it works.

One of the side effects to this is that it not only helps you take some of the fire out of the situation, it also restores some of your pride and self-respect. When you are not totally dominated and controlled, it is a big thing. It is one of the things that is going to help you to start feeling good about yourself again. All of the things that we have spoken about in this section are designed to make you start thinking for yourself and about yourself. Once you are doing this you are then able to start feeling better about yourself, and you will also start seeing the light at the end of the tunnel, it may still be a long way off, but once all of the myths and lies have been removed it is much easier to see it.

Control is in the mind; make sure it is only in the abusers mind.

By the way this does not only apply to victims and their abusers; it applies to all people in all situations. Doing something out of choice, rather than because you have to makes a very big difference.

DEALING WITH FEAR

Throughout the rest of this book apart from control the other main feature for the victim is fear. I have talked extensively about fear and the effects it can have. I have talked about how fear is not rational and that it only has to be believed to be real. Here I am going to talk about a simple way of dealing with the fears. Again this is general, and you need to take the concept and the idea and apply it to your situation.

Fear is a great deal more complex than I am able to explain in this book, and there is a lot more to dealing with it than I am able to talk about here also, but there is one method of dealing with fear that I use and I find it to be quite simple and very effective.

When you are thinking about something that you are afraid of, (for whatever reason) the key to being able to face and conquer it is to ask yourself some simple questions.

Firstly you have to identify the object of your fear. A lot of the fears that I have spoken about in this book do not necessarily surface when you are living in the middle of it unless you sit down and analyse things critically in the way that I have done here.

Then what you have to do is to try and reason through the fear. Some of the fears can be ruled out because they are really not going to happen. A fear of the abuser winning custody of the children for example, that is very unlikely to happen when you really think about it, so it is not really something that you need to worry about too much. There may be battles etc. that you will have to deal with, but think about the whole thing and see if that is really something that is likely to happen.

If you cannot beat the fear by critically analysing it, then the next thing you need to think about is what is the worst thing that can possibly happen?

You do have to try and be realistic about this. You have to be reasonable when you are answering this question and you have to try and be as specific as you can.

Once you have decided what the worst thing that can happen is, the next question you need to ask yourself is; could you cope if that were to happen?

Again you have to be realistic about this; you have to know what you could and could not cope with. You will find that people can cope with a lot more than they realise. Just take your situation for example; you are coping with all that.

If you decide that you could cope with the worst thing that could happen, then although it may not be ideal and it may not be pleasant, there is really no reason why you need to let the fear stop you, or even worry you.

The next thing to do, if you are still not sure that you can face the thing that you are afraid of is to think about what is the worst thing that can happen if you do not do it, and you let the fear stop you?

Once you have decided what the worst thing for not doing something is, then you need to decide if you could cope with that scenario.

The next step then is to compare both of the worst case scenarios, and decide which one you want to face.

What this does is make you stop and think about things and also gives you options to consider and weigh against each other. You need to consider the consequence of each option, as far as you understand it, and then decide the best course of action.

This same technique can also be used to help you deal with the things that are worrying you. Worry is something that we do by taking a known situation, think that the worst case scenario is going to happen and then we let it bother us. Firstly you need to decide if you can cope with the worst thing that can happen. If you could cope with it, then you will cope with it IF it happens.

The other thing when it comes to worry is to ask yourself if there is anything that you can do to change the outcome of something that is worrying you. If the answer is no, then there is nothing that you can do, and stressing about it not going to help, no matter how much you do. I have never seen or heard of stress and worry solving a problem, never.

As I said this is something simple, but effective. You will also notice that again it is just about adjusting the way that you are thinking about things. I cannot emphasize enough how important the way you think is. It is perhaps the most important and powerful aspect of a person's life. Once you can control the way that you think, and when you can think about things in a number of different ways, then you can do anything you want.

The human mind is the core of the person. I know some people will say that soul is the core of the person, and whilst that is also true, it is the mind that we use to control how we think, which directly affects how we feel, and how we think and feel essentially dictates how we act. It is how we act or what we do that decides for the most part how our lives are going to unfold.

Think about the things you are afraid of, and think about the options of doing it or not doing it then make an informed choice. Do not blindly dismiss something just because you are afraid, you are just creating a barrier and removing options, and that is all bad.

FIVE YEARS FROM NOW

In the section directed to the abuser, I talked about considering the path that they are on and where it is leading or where they are going to be five years from now. I am going to talk to you about doing this here also. It is an important exercise to do because it forces you to step back from the day to day and think about where your life is heading.

I have talked about how life carries us along like a conveyor belt, whether we like it or not and whether we know it or not we are going to end up somewhere. We pass through many different stages in our journey of life even though at times it seems like things never change; that one day is the same as the next, but that is not really true.

There are things changing around us all of the time, it may not directly affect us or have a major impact that we notice straight away, but it is all the little changes that are going on that culminate and affect us in major ways somewhere along the way.

A great example of this is the abusive relationship that you are now living in. This is something that did not just start, or if it did, it is still something that progressed through time and got a little worse and before you knew it, here you are. Life has a habit of sneaking up on people and unless you actually take a moment and take a step back and have a look from the outside, so to speak, then life just sort of gradually happens to you a little at a time and it is not possible to retrace your steps.

That is the thing with life, there is no way of re-living the past, and there is no way of changing the things that have already happened. Once it is done, it is done. The key thing is to be aware of what is happening before it gets to the point of regret then you do have a chance of changing things.

I am going to give you a couple of things to think about with this little exercise and guide you through it a little. Below are a few options, consider each one and then think about where it is will take you in the next five years.

Option one

Consider your current situation and how it has progressed over the last five years, and then how it is likely to be in the next five years if things continue on their present course.

If there are children in the relationship you also need to take them into account based on the way you are with them and the way your home life is. These are all critical to how they are going to grow over the next five years.

When you do this you need to be as precise as you can. Think about the house, the area that you will be living in. Think about your relationship with your partner, and how they are most likely going to be treating you in five years time.

Think about you and how you are going to be in five years and what you are going to be doing. Are you still going to be the same as you are now, are you going to still be clinging on the edges of the dark hole that you seem to be stuck in?

Now ask yourself, is that what you really want for you? If there are kids, is that what you really want for them?

Option two

With this option I want you to think about things a bit differently. I want you to think about how it will be in five years time if you were to take the advice and information that is offered in this book.

If you were to become a different person and you are able to break free of the abusive relationship that you are in. You need to be as honest as you can with this. I do not want you going back to the ideal world scenario that we talked about earlier. I want you to think about things in the real world.

I want you to realise that in order for to break free of the relationship, it is going to come with its own set of problems and hassles.

There are a couple of things that you need to take into consideration here. Firstly for you to break free of the relationship you are going to become a slightly different person to who you are now. You are going to have to get some self-respect and dignity. You are going to have to get stronger and you are going to have to stop tolerating the treatment that you have been getting until now.

This option is a bit harder than the previous one, because it takes a bit of a leap of faith to be able to do it.

If there are children involved you need to take them into consideration also. How are they going to be, and where are they going to be after the changes are made?

Keep in mind the long term effects of this; not just the immediate pain and stress that it is going to cause.

Now that you have done this, you need to compare this to the first one and see how different they are.

Now ask yourself, which is the better option?

Other options

There are a few other options that you can also consider.

What if the abuse were to escalate beyond what it is now? Chances are that it will get progressively worse. Nothing stays the same and that includes the level of abuse. Rarely does it get less.

What if the abuse switches from you to the children?

What will happen if you decide to leave?

What is the financial situation going to be like in both cases?

What if at some point the abuse finally breaks you?

What if you grow enough to really get on with your life?

What if you get a job, or go to college?

What if you meet someone else?

The point of this exercise is to at least start thinking about the future and to also recognise the path that you are on. I am not suggesting that you do anything other than think about these things. Think about where you want to be in your life in five years time and think about where you will be if you keep doing what you are doing.

I am not in a position to offer advise except to say that you can make a difference to yourself, even in the current environment, and you can think about where it is all taking you. It is up to you to decide what you do with the things that I tell you here.

HOW DO YOU MAKE THE MOVE?

This chapter is not about me giving you a set of steps or even suggestions to follow to break out of your relationship. I think I have made it very clear that I simply cannot do that in this medium.

What this chapter is about is the different ways that you can break out of a relationship and what it can mean to you, as a person, in the longer term.

There are a number of different ways to break free of an abusive relationship, and they all come with their own pitfalls and dangers. But how you actually make the break is going to effect you and your life from that moment on.

I am sure there are many other variations to the ones that I am going to talk about, and once again please note that I am talking generally and I am not offering advice or suggestions that you should do any of them particularly.

Firstly the one that I want to talk about is the literal packing of the car in the middle of the night, or during the day when the abuser is away and making a run for it. I know there are times when this is called for, and once again I am not advocating its use or non use, I am simply talking about it in terms of the effect it has on the victim (now fugitive), in the longer term.

The problem with this method is that the person that does this is essentially going to be living in fear. This is almost like someone breaking out of prison. It is an effective method of getting away, and whilst it does take a great deal of courage to do this, given the circumstances that cause someone to do this, it also leaves the victim in an almost constant state of fear. For someone to move on after an event like this takes a huge shift in thinking; they have to restart their lives from nothing. Not to mention the constant fear and looking over the shoulder that comes with it.

The next method is where the police are involved and the

abuser is arrested and removed. This also takes a great deal of courage to do. It is not an easy thing to go through, and there are also no guarantees that the abuser is going to be imprisoned. That means that they are going to be around the place, and they are going to be a constant threat.

The third method is a situation in which the victim leaves the abuser of their own free will. What this requires is for the victim to re-invent themselves as a person whilst still in the relationship. The thing with doing it this way is that not only does it prove to the victim that they are better than they have been treated, it also sends a very clear message to the abuser that the victim is not going to be intimidated or bullied by them anymore.

It does not mean that the abuser is simply going to go away and that things are all going to be rosy, but it does mean that the victim is in a better place within themselves when the move actually happens.

I want to be absolutely crystal clear on this point. I am not suggesting that one method is better than the other and I am not suggesting that you should seek to do one or the other at any time in your relationship. I am simply putting them out there as options and to illustrate a point.

The point that I am trying to make here is that there are different ways to do things. It depends very much on the people involved and the situation, it is not for me to say or recommend anyone of them.

I do want to talk more about the state of mind when the break is actually made. I think that it is important to understand that whatever way you do break free of your relationship, it is your state of mind when you make the break that is crucial.

If you take the first example here, then the first thought is that the victim is in a state of fear and is reacting to a worsening situation; however this does not have to be true. This sort of move may be the only way that someone can physically get away. If you have a valid reason for choosing this option then maybe it is okay.

Once again I point back to the visit to the dentist; the reason that we do something changes the way we think about it and the way that it can affect us going forward. Someone who makes this move because they have come out of the haze of being a victim and has planned this move, is actually taking control of their lives, perhaps for the first time in a long time, and therefore going forward they are going to much better for it.

The person, who runs out of fear and panic, is still thinking and feeling like a victim, and therefore going forward with their life is going to be difficult as they are still stuck in the haze of lies and barriers that has held them captive for so long.

The same applies to the other options mentioned above. It all comes down to the state of mind of the person making the move. This is the main issue. It is not the method so much as the state of mind of the person that is making the move.

This is quite evident when you look at how many people return to an abusive relationship even after they have broken free. It is because they may have broken free physically, but they have not broken free mentally and emotionally and they are still thinking of themselves as a victim and therefore they return, even knowing that it is going to be worse than it ever was.

There are a lot of different ways to physically achieve the same objective and that is breaking out of the relationship, but it is the state of mind and the way of thinking that needs to be right in order to make progress.

I do want to say that it does take a tremendous amount of strength and courage to break out of any abusive relationship, regardless of your state of mind or the method that you use. The more control you have over it, the better, but please think it through before doing anything like this. There are consequences and you should be prepared for whatever might come, regardless of what they are.

Once again I am not suggesting that someone who is not mentally strong should simply remain in an abusive relationship, what I am saying is that it is better to be in a stronger frame of mind. I am not suggesting that just because you are feeling better and stronger after reading this book that you should just pack up and leave. I am not making any suggestions about what you should or shouldn't do about your current situation, I am merely suggesting ways that you can change you thinking, and therefore change your view of things. I am not recommending anything other than you think about things and see if you can make it better for you.

WHAT HAPPENS AFTER THE MOVE?

I am now going to be talking to you about what happens to you after you do break free of the relationship. As I have already said a lot depends on your state of mind when you do leave the relationship, but I am going to write this chapter for everyone. I am assuming that if you are reading this it is because you are thinking of changing your situation in the first place, and I am assuming that you have read all of the good stuff that has preceded this chapter.

The first thing that I want to say is congratulations. To break free is a great thing to do and I know it is one of the hardest things you have to do, but I do think it will be worth it. You have effectively saved your life. Maybe not in the literal sense, but as a person you have saved your life.

Once you get out of an abusive relationship the world can be a very daunting place. All of the things that you held onto during the relationship that made you feel secure are not the same. For a start you might have to live in a different place and things are now all very different.

It may be the first time in years that you have to take control over your life and you have to worry about things that perhaps the abuser has always handled. Once again it is how you approach this that is going to make a big difference.

If you can approach it as a new start and an adventure then you will be able to move and adapt to things a lot quicker. If you approach it as though you have been dropped onto a strange planet and the best thing for you to do is to hide away and remain in survival mode, then you are going to struggle.

If you have broken free because it is something that you wanted to do and it is something that you planned to happen then you will have already thought about some of the things that you want to do and will already have an idea of where you are going with your life.

On the other hand if this is something that you had not prepared for and you are still not sure that you have done the right thing, then you need to start thinking in terms of what you are going to do with your life now. The sooner you can snap out of victim mode the easier it is going to be.

The thing with making the break is that it is a chance for a whole new beginning. You can leave the person that was the victim for all those years behind you. You now have the opportunity to live your life the way that you want it.

If you can think about the fact that you have broken free and therefore have had the shackles removed you will be able to approach the new life in a different way.

I am not going to tell you that simply breaking out physically and even growing mentally and emotionally mean that you are just going to forget about the past. This has been a part of your life for a long period of time, and it is not all going to disappear overnight.

I know that it has been four years since Ange took the action to break out of her relationship, and even now there are still times that she has flashbacks. There are still times when the automated responses that developed during that time still show up. Although we have a very different environment than it was, it is still a part of our lives, and will be for a number of years to come yet. These things have got less and less as time has gone on, and they do not have a huge impact, if any, on our lives, but they are still there nonetheless.

One of the things that you will have to deal with is a certain amount of guilt. After all you were the one that ended the relationship. It does not make sense when you see it here, but that is the way it works.

There will also be certain amount of anger and rage. After all, that person mistreated you for all of those years; obviously you are going to be angry about it.

There will be a lot of fear. All of the fears that we talked about throughout this book do not suddenly disappear. Not to mention the fear of the abuser and the retribution that may or may not come.

There are going to be nightmares and there are going to be flashbacks.

There are going to be times when you doubt yourself as a person and there are times that you are going to question whether you did the right thing or not. Now you start to see why some people return to the relationship.

But the thing that you need to do through all of those doubts and questions is to keep pushing forward with your life. You have a new life now, you can do what you want, think what you want, see who you want and go where you want to go.

The sooner you can settle into something more permanent the better. It will help you to feel safe and secure and you will be able to launch your new life from a safe place.

Most importantly think about what it was like before and think about what it would be like to go back to living like that. As frightening and scary as the present is and the future is, it has to be better than returning to where you have come from.

I did mention earlier that there is no way to turn the clock back. The same applies to the abuser, they are not going to turn the clock back; they are going to be worse than ever, regardless of what they tell you.

If you do think about going back then think back to all the reasons that you decided to leave in the first place. Those reasons have not gone away and that should keep you away. Go forward not backward.

We are going to talk a little more about going forward and not backward in the next chapter, but for now you should be proud of yourself for having the courage to break free, and you should hang on to that courage and the fact that it was actually you that found that courage in the first place. It was there within you then and it will be there for you to go forward.

MOVING OUT HAS TO MEAN MOVING ON

When I talk about moving on I am not only talking about moving on from the relationship, I am also talking about moving on as a person from the person that was the victim and moving on with your life.

As I said earlier the past is not all of a sudden going to disappear and a new person is not suddenly going to appear either. There is still a lot of work to be done on the person in order to make sure that you can keep moving forward.

An abusive relationship does take something away from a person and whilst I have given you some things to help with that, there are still a lot of things to do.

One of the things that you will need to do at some stage is to make sure that you leave the past behind you. You cannot keep being a victim and you cannot keep dragging all of the bad things that have happened to you in the past with you. You have to leave them behind.

You have to be careful that you do not assume what I call the 'poor me' personality. This is the person that rolls out the terrible past and almost clings onto it in order to justify why they have not moved on with their life. This is the person that has a ready made excuse for everything because of what they had to go through for years.

There are also the people that will try to move on but for some reason cannot leave the past behind. It is something that seems to stay with them and they almost constantly remind themselves of it, not because they are looking for attention or because they are using it as an excuse but they have come to believe that they need to resolve some things about it all and until they can do that, they cannot leave it behind them.

Think of life as being made up of a series of moments in time, which it literally is. When you get down to it there is only the present moment that you can actually do anything with. All of the moments that have gone in the past cannot be changed. You can analyse them, you can try and understand them, you can even try to sift through them to find some meaning for all the things that have happened, but ultimately the only thing that you can do with the past is to learn from it.

You do not have to carry it with you everywhere you go in order to learn from it. It is something that you can do at times, and then at some point you simply have to put it behind you and let it go.

Here is another metaphor for you think about. Think about your life in terms of a ladder. The future is up ahead of you and what you need to do to get on with your future is to keep climbing the ladder. However if you have all of the past in a big bag over your shoulder you are going to find it very difficult, if not impossible to climb the ladder into the future. If you do manage to keep climbing then by the time you get to the future the rest of world has moved on. If you don't manage to climb the ladder because you are trying to drag all of your past with you, then you are simply going to stay behind and live in the past. That is not what you want; if you wanted to live in the past then you would not have made the move in the first place.

Learn from the past, so that you do not make the same mistakes again, then put it down and leave it behind. It is too heavy to take forward with you, at best it will slow you down and at worst it will bring you to a grinding halt, and you will still be trapped there.

In the previous chapter I talked about how a lot of people will finally get the courage, or be afraid enough to finally break free and then will return to the abuser and therefore the abuse. There could be many reasons for this but it is something that I think that we need to talk about. Part of it has to do with the state of mind and the amount of preparation that has taken place before the break is made. When you are stuck in an abusive relationship it does become a bit like a cocoon, and you are almost separated from the rest of the world. I have talked about comfort zones previously, and as bad as the abuse is, it is still a comfort zone in that it is the place that you know. Remember a comfort zone does not have to be an ideal place, it does not even have to be safe; it just has to be familiar enough for you to want to stay there.

Then all of a sudden all of those things are removed. The day to day trials of life are not removed. The fear is not removed, the doubt is not removed and it is not necessarily a re-birthing experience. It is scary, pure and simple, and it can even be scary enough to force you to return to the very place that you have broken free from.

I am sure that everyone has heard about prisoners that are serving long sentences and finally get released, only to break the law again, almost immediately, simply because they do not know how to survive in the outside world, and this really is no different.

There is no shame in doing this. You may be blaming yourself for staying so long in the first place, and then if you are to return you hate yourself even more, because even though you finally got out, you went back. Now you really think that you have chosen this life for yourself, and I am sure there are people that will tell you exactly that. But please do not give up. Just because it has not worked for you in the past does not mean that it is not going to work for you in the future. Remember that the past is the past, and you cannot turn back the clock. Learn from what happened in the past, try and understand it as much as you can, so that next time you are a little wiser about the whole thing and you can do it better.

The other thing that is quite common is that someone will break free of an abusive relationship and then meet someone else and form a new relationship which turns out to be abusive also. I think that this, and the previous example, are both related to the state of mind of the person at the time. They are still thinking and feeling like a victim. They have not made the change from being a victim to being a person who was the victim of a situation. It is a big distinction and it can have a major impact on what happens.

There is one thing that I do recommend, even if you think that you have it all under control and that is to seek help. There is a huge amount of help available, and even though you are not in the relationship any more do not be afraid to get help and support to make sure that you keep moving forward, and do not go backwards to the 'safety' of the comfort zone.

Throughout life there are many times when we need help with various things and there is certainly no shame with seeking help when we need it. Nobody knows everything, and nobody has all of the answers. There is always someone who can give you a little more understanding and a different view on things, make use of as much of the help as you can.

There is one thing that I will say about seeking help and that is not to become too reliant on it. The sooner you learn to stand on your own two feet, and become the person that you want to become, the better it will be for you. The abuser has made you dependant on them for a number of years and it is very easy to transfer that dependence to someone or something else. This is a very easy trap to fall into and one that you should be aware of. Always go back to thinking for yourself and taking responsibility for yourself and your action. You may not always control the situation and you can't always control the things that have and will happen to you, but you can always control how you respond to them, and that is by controlling you, how you think and what you do.

The title of this chapter says that moving out has to mean moving on. It is critical that you do try your hardest to move on with your life, and the sooner you do it the better it will be for you. I am not talking about the physical; I am talking about moving on within yourself. The sooner you stop being the victim and thinking like the victim the better you will be for it.

Try and focus on the future, and not the past. Always be

thinking forward and not backwards. Be thinking as a person and not a victim.

Don't forget where you have come from to get to where you are now, and don't forget what you have had to go through to get to where you are now. Think about what it took for you to get to where you are now. Regardless of the type of abuse and severity of the abuse, it does take a huge leap of faith for you to be able to break free of it, and you should always remind yourself that it is a huge achievement and it is something that you should be proud of.

When you do look back, look back with pride and not self-pity, because you need to focus on what it took to break free, not how bad it was and how hard it was for you. Don't wear your suffering as a badge of honour, wear your pride and success with honour.

The flashbacks, nightmares and fears will lessen over time. It is not going to happen instantly and it is not something that you should beat yourself up over. You will be able to trust again, and you will move on, a little at a time. Trust me on that one.

Onwards and upwards, forwards not backwards.

REVENGE IS NOT THE ANSWER

I don't think that I need to explain the title of this chapter very much. Not because it is pretty obvious what it is about, but because I am sure there are not too many that break free that do not want to get some kind of revenge on the abuser. It is pretty much human nature to want to settle old scores. I know that it can be infuriating when you think of that all the pain and all the suffering that someone inflicted on you without paying the penalty.

I completely understand that you feel that way. Considering what they did to you, and the other thing is that chances are they are going to go on and do it to someone else, and that sort of upsets you as well.

The thing with revenge is that it comes from two things, and they are anger and hate. You want to get even because you are angry with the abuser for what they did to you and you more than likely hate them and want to do something just to make yourself feel better.

There are many reasons why wanting and seeking revenge is not the answer but the key reason is that it is not really going to help you. Sure making the abuser feel bad may make you feel good, but in the bigger picture it is not really going to add anything to your life, in fact the whole time you are thinking like this you are taking something away from your new life.

All the time you are thinking about revenge and thinking about how angry you are and how much you hate the abuser, you are living in the past. It is for the past that you want retribution; you could even say that you are looking for something to compensate yourself for all the crap that you had to go through. While you are continually thinking like this, you are living in the past; and while you are living in the past you cannot be living in the present and you most certainly are not moving forward.

I am going to tell you something that I hope will make you feel differently about the abuser and I hope it will help you to forget your need for revenge, and then you can leave the past where it belongs; behind you.

Let's have a look at where you are now. Since you broke free of the relationship your life has moved on. It may not be ideal, but you have moved on. You now do the things that you want to do. You are free to be who you are and you are free to think for yourself. You may even have met someone else, who treats you right. The point is, you and your life have moved on, and things are certainly a lot better than they once were. You have learnt and grown from the experience and you may even be a better person because of it. You are no longer living in constant fear, and you are just getting on with things, except for this need for revenge.

On the other hand let's look at the abuser. They are still angry and they are still filled with hate. They may have found someone else, and chances are sooner or later they are going to go back to who they really are. They are still looking for someone to blame for all of the bad things in their life. They are still manipulating and they are still controlling. As much as leaving turned your life upside down, it did the same to them. Chances are they are still filled with rage and hate that is directed at you.

And here is the thing, you have moved on with your life, they are still miserable and angry and nasty, and chances are they are never going to change that. You know when someone is like that; there is no way that they can be happy. You simply cannot be happy when you are living your life in that way.

When you start to look at it that way; maybe it is pity you should be feeling for the abuser, because they are still a bitter, twisted and nasty individual, and you have moved on. What are you going to do to them to make them any more miserable?

To be honest it would be better for you not to feel anything towards the abuser, they do not even deserve your anger and they do not deserve your pity. The less you think about them, even if it is plotting or wishing to get revenge on them, the better it is for you and your new life.

You worked hard to get this person out of your life, every moment that you spend thinking about them; you are simply inviting them back into your life. Do you really want that person in your new life?

I would suggest that you absolutely do not, so stop bringing them into it by thinking about them and spending your time feeling angry and bitter towards them. Save your energy for the good things in your current life and the good things that will be coming your way, don't waste it on them; they are simply not worth it.

The whole point of moving on is leaving the past in the past and that includes the desire for revenge. Either way you look at it, the abuser and what they did is in the past, and it is not something that you want to keep dragging with you. Leave it where it belongs, behind you. You do not need it.

The other thing that a lot of people talk about is that they feel the need to understand why the abuser did what they did. You know, it does not matter to you why they did what they did. You do not need to analyse them to live your life. Ultimately the reason they did what they did is something for them to worry about, it is not something that you need to focus on. You need to worry about you and why you did what you did, so that you can learn from your mistakes to make sure that you do not make them again.

You know you probably are never going to be able to justify what the abuser did or why they did it, and it simply does not matter.

People spend far too much time worrying about what everyone else is doing and far too less time worrying about what they are doing and why they are doing it. It is you that you must to spend your time thinking about and it is you that you need to spend your time improving. I am not talking about being selfish or anything like that; I am talking about worrying about the things that you can change and have a positive impact on. The best thing you can do for yourself is becoming a better person so that you can help someone else who may need you at some point.

Leave it behind you as much as you can. Leave the anger and pity and the need to understand in the past. Understand yourself and what you did, but leave the abuser to do their self-analysis, and leave them to wallow in their anger and misery.

The best revenge that you can possibly get is to get on with your new life and make the most of it. Nothing will annoy the abuser more than seeing you prosper. Think about that every time you win and when things are going well for you; that is all the revenge that you need.

ARE THEY STILL CONTROLLING YOUR LIFE?

I suppose this question could also be are you still living like a victim? Do you still spend all of your time thinking about how bad it was for you? Do you still look over your shoulder wondering if the abuser is still there or is going to show up? Do you still live in fear?

I am not talking about the flashbacks and the nightmares, and I am not talking about the rational fear that may be necessary, what I am talking about is what is going on inside your mind.

One of the things that can happen is that the fear and doubt can still control you. You can still spend your time thinking that you are not deserving of your new life. Even if your new life is not all rosy, and let's be honest here, nobody's ever is, but even if it is not working exactly as you had planned, it has got to be better than it was before. The very fact that you are free from the abuser has got to mean that your life is a lot better than it was when you were still trapped.

What happens is that the fear and doubt are still so ingrained in you that you tend to focus on the bad things that are going on in your life, you are almost afraid to have the good things because you are always scared that at any moment the bubble is going to burst and you are going to be dragged back into the past. This is not an unusual way of thinking and feeling, but it is something that you should try to deal with.

When you are still living like this and you are still living in fear and doubt, you are still living as though the abuser is still in your life and is still controlling the way you think. Even though they may not be a part of your life anymore, they are still controlling you to a certain degree.

When you finally get out of an abusive relationship there is not a switch that you can just flick that is going to mean that all of these things are going to go away, and I am not going to tell you that I have the magic words that will make them all go away for you.

Even four years after Ange broke free of her abuser, and moved on with her life there are still times when she has the little automatic triggers that go off that make her react in the same way as she did when he was still controlling her. She calls it her little implant; that little thing that is in the back of the mind where the flashbacks and the nightmares come from; the little voice that still gets to her at times. Over time this has had less and less effect, but it is still there.

These things do not go away over night, but the point is what you do when they come. If you react to them in the same way that you reacted to them when the abuser was still there, when you let them stop you from moving forward with your life and doing the things that you wanted to do, then they are still controlling you. The abuser still has control over you, and therefore your life and also anyone else that is still a part of your life.

There are going to be times when you go through what I call 'Pity Parties'. They are the times when you are feeling down and feeling sorry for yourself, and you are wallowing in your misery and the unfairness of the situation and how bad your life has been and how badly you have been treated. I am sure you know what I am talking about. We all do it, abused or not, we all have pity parties.

The thing with these moments is that when they come it is important to have the pity party, and it is also important that you come out of it pretty quickly. If you spend your life in a pity party and you spend your life as a victim then you are quite simply still being controlled by the abuser.

The worse part about it is the abuser doesn't even know they have that control and to be quite honest they don't even care. It is not that they have control; it is that you do not. It all comes back to your state of mind and what you spend your time thinking about. If you are still thinking and living like a victim, then you are still a victim; it is as simple as that.

All the time you spend thinking about the abuser and the abuse and every time you allow it to stop you from moving on with your life you are giving control to the abuser and that is not what you want to do. The worst thing is; it is not just your life that you are allowing to be controlled by the abuser it is the people around you that you are allowing the abuser to control also.

You see the way that this works is that if you allow the past to control the way you do things then you are causing the people around you to also be trapped in your past. Because what you are doing has an effect on them. I know that this is something that has at times happened with Ange and I. There are times when it seems to me that I am paying someone else's debt. None of this is intentional and generally we talk it through and Ange realises what is happening and then we work around it.

Like I said, these things do not go away, just because you have broken free. The amount of mental and emotional damage is not something that can be measured, there is no instant cure.

The key is to try and recognise it when it comes and try to work through it.

Half the battle with these things is being aware of them in the first place and also not to underestimate the effect that being a victim in an abusive relationship can have on you.

Do not be hard on yourself just because these things are still in your head and just because it has not all disappeared over night. The trick is to know that it is happening, deal with it when it does, and make sure you move on. Don't allow it to overwhelm you and keep you as a victim and in a pity party forever.

It is critical that you do deal with them, and it is important that when they do come, you do confront them. Do not just push them away and effectively hide from them, confront them and deal with them. They are only memories and thoughts, they cannot hurt you, but they can control you if you allow them to.

THINK AND GROW

I have spoken a lot about how it is important to look at the way that you think, and I believe that I have given enough examples that show just how important it is.

Sadly people do not spend enough time or pay enough attention to what is going on inside their minds. It is easy not to, it is easy just to get caught up in the day to day of life, and let it sort of roll you along, and unless something happens you never actually ever stop to think about it.

Just as the relationship and abuse is one of those things that just sort of happened along the way, so does everybody's lives. It is rare that someone will actually stop and think about what they are doing, where they are going and most importantly what it is they are thinking about.

I am reemphasising this because it is an important thing and it will change your life if you let it. Even if you do nothing different except to change the way you think, things will change for you.

Continue with the things that I have talked about throughout this book, continue to focus on what you are thinking and how you are thinking and continue to work on you as a person.

Keep thinking and keep growing, that is the key to getting the things that you want in life. Think about what it is that you want, grow into the person you need to be to get the things you want and then go for it.

There is a self-help book that has been around for a number of years and it is called 'Think and Grow Rich', and it has sort of become a catch phrase, but I like to change it to say something like...

Think and Grow... Whatever you want ...

That is the way to a successful and happy life; do not leave it to chance.

END OF SECTION

Throughout this section I have been focussing directly on the victim and about where they are and who they are. It is very easy to lose who they are when it is constantly taken away from them and is replaced by the thoughts and wishes of someone else.

Even if they are still stuck in an abusive relationship it does not mean that they have to surrender control of everything to the abuser. Our thoughts are exactly that – ours. Unless we choose to allow someone else to control our thoughts they are the one thing that we truly can call our own.

How we think and what we spend our time thinking about can change a lot about our lives. It may not change the situation and it is not going to make the abuse stop, but it does help to keep the person as a person and not a victim. They may be the victim, but they do not have to become a victim.

Simply changing the way that we think and therefore changing the reason that we do something makes the whole thing very different. When we do something because we choose to do it, instead of because we have to do it, then it becomes much more bearable. At the same time it still means that the person is still kept as an individual and it is the individual that will need to gather the strength and courage to break free of the abuse.

I have also talked about how being in an abusive relationship is like living in a haze. That haze is created by the control and the myths that the abuser creates for the victim. We looked at some of those myths and hopefully explained them in such a way as to remove them as barriers for the victim.

The primary focus of this chapter has been about changing the way that we think. If you change that, then you are well and truly on the road to rediscovering the person and that is the first step to recovery.

I do want to point out one more time, that I do not want to put anyone in danger and I do not want to create more problems for the victim. All of the examples I used here are purely that, examples. I make no other recommendations other than to start changing the person, by changing your thought patterns. I do not know anything about your situation, and the information is provided to be general and is to provide you with ideas that you can take and apply to your situation.

THE LAST BIT

At the end of the day

Wow, what a journey it has been to get through this book. To be honest it was only as I started writing this that I realised that I had so much to say on this subject.

Reading this book is not going to solve any of your problems unless you actually use the information in it. Knowledge is power, but power is useless if it lies dormant and is not used. It is up to you as to how much you get out of this book, and it is up to you what you do with the information that I have provided you with here. I can only do so much, but it has to come back to you the individual to actually take the steps and do something with what you know.

This has been a very tough book to write, and I hope that I have done the subject justice. My aim with writing this book is not only to help those that are in an abusive relationship, it is also to provide information that looks beneath the surface and I have tried to explain the complexities as plainly as I can.

I know that when I started to look into this subject in a little more detail it was the complexities that really surprised me. I always work on the theory that we are all responsible for who we are and where we are, and whilst I still think that is true, it has given me a new understanding of that, in that sometimes when we make our choices, we do not always anticipate the consequences and we can get caught in something that we simply do not know how to get out of.

I have tried to be as non-judgmental as I can, and I have tried to be as gender neutral as I can and I think for the most part I have been pretty successful with that.

Now that you have a good general understanding of this subject, I hope that it will help you to make a difference, either to your life, or to the life of someone you are trying to help. I am always interested in receiving feedback. If there is anything you would like to talk to me about, then please email me at brian@smellthereality.com

I wish you all the luck and good fortune in the world. Please keep thinking and keep moving forward. I am going to leave you with a quote from Deepak Chopra that I think is the best way to sum it up and I hope that you will take this message with you wherever you go and wherever your life takes you.

"Every time you are tempted to react in the same old way, ask yourself if you want to be a prisoner of the past or a pioneer of the future. The past is closed and limited; the future is open and free."